English for Global Business

An Intermediate-Level Course

Emily Lites and Kathy Thorpe

Ann Arbor

THE UNIVERSITY OF MICHIGAN PRESS

Contact the authors at:
lites@bizenglish.com
and
kathythorpe@compuserve.com

Contents

English for Global Business, Intermediate Level
Scope and Sequence

Module and Unit	Listening Tasks	Functional Language	TOEIC® Tip	Professional Protocol
Module 1. Getting Acquainted 1. Introducing Yourself 2. Introducing Others 3. Starting a Conversation 4. Ending a Conversation and Leave-taking	Catching Names and Titles Matching Introductions with Business Cards Following the Conversation Listening for Questions	Introductions Greetings Conversation Gambits Asking Follow-up Questions Pre-Endings and Endings	Tag Questions for Verification and Conversation	Guidelines for Introductions in the United States
Module 2. Describing Your Work 5. Talking about Facts and Figures 6. Introducing Your Company 7. Describing Company Organization 8. Describing Job Responsibilities	Catching Names and Percentages Understanding and Using Facts and Figures Understanding Company Information, History and Organizational Structure Understanding Job Titles and Responsibilities	Saying Numbers, Decimals, Percentages and Fractions Talking about Money Presenting Company Information Describing Products and Services, the Workforce, and Revenue Discussing Departments and Lines of Authority Describing a Typical Day	Use of the Passive Voice	Guidelines for Presentations in the United States
Module 3. Telephoning 9. Problems Telephoning 10. Making a Phone Call 11. Scheduling a Meeting 12. Ending a Phone Conversation	Understanding Telephone Conversations Listening for Key Words Taking Messages Understanding Phone Answering Machine Messages Making Appointments	Asking to Speak to Someone and Stating the Purpose of the Call Taking Messages Setting up a Meeting or Appointment Confirming Plans Ending Phone Calls	Everyday Conversational Language Identifying Logical Answers	Guidelines for Making Telephone Calls in English
Module 4. Traveling Internationally 13. Making Plans 14. Making Airline Reservations 15. Booking a Hotel, Checking In, and Checking Out 16. Describing Products at a Trade Show	Distinguishing Large and Small Differences Understanding the Airline Ticketing Agent Understanding a Travel Agent and Front Desk Clerk	Discussing Plans Talking about Similarities and Differences Asking for Flight Information Asking about Travel Plans Making a Hotel Reservation, Checking in and Out Describing Products	Comparisons and Superlatives Talking about Large and Small Differences Quantitative Comparisons	Guidelines for Using Business Cards in the United States
Module 5. Entertaining a Business Associate 17. A Business Lunch 18. Ordering Food 19. Ordering Drinks 20. Etiquette in Social Situations	Understanding Phone Answering Machine Invitations Understanding the Waitperson Listening for Speaker Attitude	Inviting a Colleague to Lunch or Dinner Making Reservations Understanding the Waitperson and the Menu Ordering Food and Drinks Social Niceties and Small Talk Using Polite Language	Noncount and Count Nouns	Guidelines for Restaurant Dining in the United States
Module 6. Discussing Issues 21. Starting a Discussion 22. Giving Opinions, Agreeing, and Disagreeing 23. Developing the Discussion 24. Summarizing Views and Making Suggestions	Understanding Discussion Format Catching Main Points Identifying Fact and Opinion Understanding Tone of Voice Listening for the Speaker's View	Starting a Discussion and Leading into the Topic Giving Opinions Agreeing/Disagreeing Summarizing Views and Making Suggestions Asking for Clarification Leading a Discussion	Use of Indirect Questions	Guidelines for Discussions in the United States

To the Student

English for Global Business is an intermediate-level textbook designed for business professionals who wish to improve their English communication skills and listening comprehension. The focus is on current American usage in international and professional business settings. Program participants are invited to visit http://www.bizenglish.com/ for current articles and online activities to accompany the textbook.

The program consists of a textbook (with six Modules, Information Files, Language Notes, a Listening Script and Answer Key) and audio tapes or CD-ROMs.

For each module, the following activities and sections are provided.

Warm Up: This activity creates a context for the module and helps you assess your skills with regard to the subject of the module.

Listening: The listening section at the beginning of the unit focuses on the target language. Because each listening passage is recorded at natural speed, you may not be able to understand every word. A good strategy is to listen first for the main idea and try to identify key words. Then listen a second time and answer the questions or write the missing words in the conversation. If necessary, listen a third time. After you finish, check your answers in the Listening Script at the back of the book.

Key Language: This section highlights the target language of the unit. Repeat the expressions after the tape or your instructor focusing on pronunciation. Review how these expressions are used in the Listening section, and practice until you can use them easily.

Language Mastery: This section provides a variety of exercises to help you practice and master the material. The first few exercises are controlled and progress to more communicative practice as you move through the unit. This is where the language is solidified through meaningful and communicative practice. The focus is on natural usage in realistic business situations.

Professional Protocol: This section addresses cross-cultural issues and etiquette for common business interactions in the United States. When discussing professional protocol, you are invited to compare your customs with those in the United States and with other countries.

TOEIC® Tips: Here you can practice items of particular importance when taking the standardized exam known as the Test of English for International Communication. Try the practice exercises in this section. If you need more help, refer to the Language Notes.

Communication Activities: Each module ends with two or more communication activities that provide a chance to integrate the skills you have been practicing in a communicative way. When participating in these activities, focus on communication and meaning, but also try to use the functional language you have been studying in the module.

Listening Script and Answer Key: All listening sections are on the audio tape or CD. If the complete text is given in the unit, it will not be repeated in the Listening Script. In exercises where you are expected to check your answers, correct answers can be found in the Listening Script and Answer Key. No answers are provided for open-ended questions.

To make the greatest progress with this program:

- Review the conversations with the audio tape or CD at home. Go back and listen to the conversations without the book. When listening to a conversation, listen to a phrase, pause the recorder and say what would come next. Then listen and compare what you said to the line on the tape.
- For fluency, practice the Key Language expressions in a variety of situations: out loud by yourself, with the audio program, and with your classmates. After you can pronounce these expressions easily, you're ready to take the final step: making this language part of your regular conversations.
- Review the material you study. In order to master what you have practiced, you will need to go back and review the material on a daily basis.
- Think in English. Try to understand the main idea even if you do not know every word. If necessary, look up important words in a dictionary.
- Study frequently. If possible, review what you have studied every night.
- Pay attention to pronunciation. Listen and model what you hear on the audio tape or CD.
- Keep a notebook of new words, cultural notes and useful expressions. Review these from time to time.

To the Instructor or Trainer

English for Global Business is an English for Specific Purposes (ESP) course designed for the adult professional EFL/ESL learner who is studying English to conduct business, communicate with international professionals, advance in a career, or pursue an MBA or other university professional degree in English. In addition to people in business, those in government, law, the diplomatic corps, and related professions will find these materials particularly suitable for developing professional communication skills. This intermediate-level volume is accompanied by an audio program and emphasizes listening and speaking skills as well as current American usage in international professional settings.

Online support for instructors, including additional resources, discussion of current teaching ideas, readings and online activities, is updated regularly for the instructor at *www.bizenglish.com/*. Students can also access a variety of online activities at this site.

Prerequisites and Corequisites for This Book

Learners using these materials should already have good control of fundamental grammar and basic communicative competence in English to handle intermediate-level material. In an intensive English program setting, these books could be accompanied by grammar and (business) writing courses.

Teaching with These Materials

English for Global Business has six Modules, each with four units of study. Each Module has a theme: Getting Acquainted, Describing Your Work, Telephoning, Traveling Internationally, Entertaining a Business Associate, and Discussing Issues.

Units start with introductory and warm-up material. A listening exercise, photo, or set of discussion questions draws attention to the theme of the Module and establishes the context while giving class participants a chance to assess their skills.

After this warm-up, a Listening exercise zeros in on the functional language. Typically, participants listen two or three times to a conversation and complete a cloze version of the conversation. Then they are asked to try the conversation with a colleague.

The Key Language section highlights the functional language of each unit and allows focused practice along with the audio materials or with a partner. To gain fluency, participants need to work conscientiously with this language to achieve greater facility in speaking. Assigning review and practice of the Key Language sections for homework outside of class or in a language lab is recommended.

The Language Mastery section provides a variety of exercises designed to solidify acquisition of the functional language. Activities are graded so that the difficulty, challenge, and level of open communication increases as students move through the Language Mastery section. Due to the abundance of mid-range exercises that bridge the gap between controlled and communicative practice, this is where language is consolidated. This section challenges participants to use the functional language in a variety of exercises, activities, and tasks while focusing on natural usage in realistic, business-related situations.

The Professional Protocol section addresses cross-cultural issues and etiquette for doing business in the United States. To promote cross-cultural awareness, participants are invited to compare their customs with those in the United States and in other countries. Also included are guidelines for a variety of common social and business situations.

TOEIC Tips sections demonstrate items of particular importance when taking the standardized exam known as the Test of English for International Communication (TOEIC®), a common assessment tool in corporate settings.

The Module ends with two or more Communication Activities that provide an opportunity for extended application of the target language and give learners a chance to integrate the skills they have been practicing in a meaningful, communicative way.

At the back of the book are found additional sections: Information Files, Language Notes, a Business Etiquette Quiz based on the information provided throughout the book, and a Listening Script and Answer Key that includes answers for those items with one clear answer. Where several responses are possible, no answer is provided.

Pedagogy

The pedagogical philosophy behind the creation of these materials assumes that:

- Learners are highly motivated when the language training materials they use reflect the content and contexts they are familiar with.
- Business English materials can build from a common core of knowledge and presuppose basic familiarity with some relevant concepts. Because of an awareness of purpose, the learner's task is simplified, and the process becomes one of transferring existing knowledge into expression in English.
- Learners are actively involved in discovering their needs, selecting the most appropriate functional language, and designing role plays and communicative activities of individual relevance.
- By emphasizing the authentic tasks that professionals are required to perform on the job, language training materials can simulate the situations and tasks appropriate to the learner's profession.
- The ESP learner's purposes are functionally oriented; therefore, materials should focus on mastering the high-frequency functional language common in business and the professions.
- The gap between intellectual comprehension and accurate use of functional items is great. These materials aim to alter this disparity by providing abundant practice opportunities in authentic situations.
- Because of the short duration of specialized ESP programs, the topics, skill areas, lexical items, communicative goals, and business protocol/cultural tips are limited to those items of most benefit to the ESP learner.
- The role of the instructor using these materials is as facilitator, idea person, sounding board, co-communicator, motivator—not as an authority on business or professional life.

- Professionals whose advancement depends on performance on the TOEIC or other standardized measures of communicative ability can expect to make significant progress toward this goal by using these materials conscientiously.
- Many of the activities and language exercises throughout the books are designed with learning strategies in mind. Tips for language learning strategies are signaled to learners by use of this symbol: ➤. Following this advice is helpful in attaining the greatest progress.

Module 1

Getting Acquainted

Unit 1

Introducing Yourself

Richard Carmichael, a transportation planner in San Francisco, is flying to Paris to meet with Nicole Legrand, a representative of a French company that manufactures high-speed trains. A high-speed train route between San Francisco and Los Angeles is in the planning stage.

route: way, direction, path
stage: step in a process

Digital Vision

Digital Vision

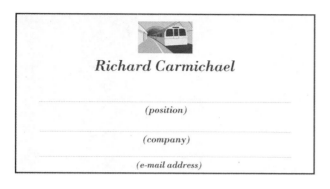

Richard Carmichael

_____
(position)

_____
(company)

_____
(e-mail address)

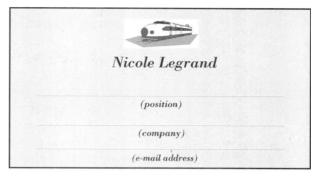

Nicole Legrand

_____
(position)

_____
(company)

_____
(e-mail address)

 Listening Practice

A. Listen and then fill in the missing information on the business cards.

B. Listen again and then answer these questions. Compare your answers with a colleague.

1. What kind of company does Nicole work for?
2. What does she do in her managerial position?
3. Why is Richard in Paris?
4. Is CalTrans going to do business with TVE?

Introductions: Assess Your Skills

1. When meeting for the first time, what greetings could you use to say "hello" to these people?

   a. a visitor from the States at your workplace   _Hello. Pleased to meet you._

   b. a company president   _____

   c. the new typist for your department _____

   d. a colleague from a competing company   _____

2. When meeting international people, what is the most difficult part of an introduction in English for you? Rate these items 1 to 5 where 1 = the most difficult and 5 = the easiest.

   a. __ understanding the names

   b. __ remembering the names

   c. __ pronouncing the names

   d. __ starting the conversation afterward

   e. __ introducing the person you've just met to someone else

Work on the skills that are most difficult for you in Module 1 to see the greatest improvement.

Listening Practice

A. This conversation between Nicole and Richard takes place at Orly Airport near Paris. The two have never met, but Nicole's sister in California plays golf with Richard and his wife. Can you understand the conversation? Listen and answer these questions by checking (✓) Nicole or Richard.

	Richard	Nicole
1. Who is the host in this situation?	❏	❏
2. Who has just arrived after a trans-Atlantic flight?	❏	❏
3. Who asks about the flight?	❏	❏

B. Before listening a second time, try to predict what the speakers will say in the blanks. Then listen and write exactly what you hear on the tape.

Carmichael: Hello, Ms. Legrand?

Legrand: _____. I'm pleased to

                meet you.

Carmichael: I'm _____ , too.

Legrand: Welcome to Paris, Mr. Carmichael._____?

Carmichael: Fine. A little long, but fine.

Legrand: Well, let's go get your bags, and then I'll take you to your hotel.

                _____.

Carmichael: Thank you. Yes, I guess I am a little tired.

C. Practice the conversation with a colleague until you can say it easily.

➤ Read each line silently. Then look at your partner when speaking.

 ## Key Language

Listen, repeat, and practice aloud with a partner.

Identifying Someone
Ms. Legrand?
You must be Mr. Carmichael.

Response
Yes, that's right.
Yes, I am.

Introducing Yourself
How do you do? I'm Nicole Legrand.
(I'm) pleased / glad / delighted to meet you.
Hello. My name's Nicole Legrand.
Hi, I'm Richard. (informal)

Greeting
How do you do? I'm Richard Carmichael.
It's a pleasure to meet you too.
Nice to meet you. I'm Richard Carmichael.
Hello, Richard. My name's Nicole.

After the Introduction	**Response**
Thank you for picking me up.	No problem. How was your flight?
It's nice to be in Paris.	Is this your first time here?
How long will you stay?	I'll be here for a week.
How long have you worked for TVE?	I've been there for nine years.

Language Mastery

 1. **Catching Names:** Listen to these self-introductions. Respond with a greeting and the name.

> *Example:*   How do you do? I'm Richard Carmichael.
> How do you do, Mr. Carmichael?

2. **Introducing Yourself:** In pairs, practice introducing yourselves. Think of something to say after the introduction. Then do the same with another colleague.

> *Example:*   A: Hello. My name is K. S. Lee. Please call me K. S.
> B: Hi, K. S. It's nice to meet you. I'm Rosa Gomez. Where are you from?

3. **Matching Activity**

> Instructor Prep Note: Photocopy File 1 (enlarge, if possible) and cut the sentences into strips to pass out.

Your instructor will give each class member one of the sentences from File 1, page 151, on a separate piece of paper. Talk to people until you find the person whose question or comment works with yours. The activity is over when everybody has found a partner.

Professional Protocol

Global Cultures

1. How do you usually greet a new professional acquaintance when you are introduced? How do you greet a good friend? Your boss? A relative?

   a. say "hello" and smile   c. shake hands   e. offer your card
   b. bow   d. kiss on the cheek or hug   f. stand up

2. Customs for introductions vary from country to country. Check the sentences that describe customs in your culture.

   a. ❑ It is important to have a firm handshake.

   b. ❑ It is best to shake hands with a light touch.

   c. ❑ Looking directly at someone is not polite when you are being introduced.

    d. ❑ It is very important to look directly at the other person when you are being introduced.

    e. ❑ People usually smile when they are introduced.

Use these Professional Protocol sections to compare customs in your country to those in the United States. (A person from the United States, for example, would check items a, d, and e above.)

Guidelines for Introductions in the United States

- Listen to the person's name and position. Repeat the name when you greet him or her.

- Smile and make eye contact when you shake hands. Stand up to show respect.

- Show respect for a visitor, client, or senior person by beginning with that person's name:

  Mr. Carmichael, I'd like you to meet Georges Bernard, our managing director. Mr. Bernard, this is Richard Carmichael from the California Department of Transportation.

  Tip: Include information about one or both people so they can begin a conversation:

  Mr. Carmichael has been working on a high-speed train project.

- The custom is to shake hands in a professional setting. In the past, a man waited for a woman to offer her hand first, but this is less common today. In the United States, a firm handshake with men and women shows strength and confidence; a weak handshake makes a bad impression.

- In the United States, people are informal and start to use first names quickly. Using first names is a sign of friendship and respect. If one person is clearly in a higher position, that person will invite the use of first names: Please call me Bob.

  Tip: Wait to use first names until asked. If everyone is using first names, do the same.

- Use titles with last names only: Mr. Shaw, Ms. Jones, ~~Ms. Mary.~~

  Tip: *Ms.* is the most common form for women in professional situations.

- Make an effort to introduce yourself and talk to new people as frequently as possible. Research shows that people who try to get acquainted with others and understand the new culture make the best progress in their language studies.

Unit 2

Introducing Others

Later that day, Mr. Carmichael has an appointment with one of the top management people at TVE International.

 Listening Practice

A. Fill in the chart as you listen to the conversation.
B. Now practice the conversation in groups of three. See the Listening Script, page 131.

Digital Vision

Person	Company or Organization	Position	Additional Information
Nicole Legrand	TVE	Manager, Marketing & Sales	Knows something about Mr. Carmichael's interests
Richard Carmichael			
Georges Bernard			

C. As the host, what other questions could Mr. Bernard ask Mr. Carmichael to keep the conversation going? Write two questions.

1. _____

2. _____

D. Practice the conversation with your colleagues again and ask your questions. Then change roles and try it again.

Key Language

Listen, repeat, and practice aloud with a partner.

Introducing Others

Formal
Mr. Carmichael, I'd like you to meet Georges
  Bernard. Georges, this is Richard Carmichael
  from CalTrans.

Informal
Sue Johnson, this is Bob Sutter.

First Speaker
How do you do? (formal and respectful)
I'm glad / pleased / delighted to meet you.
Hello. How are you today?
How're you doing?

Second Speaker
How do you do?
It's good / a pleasure to meet you too.
Just fine, thanks.
Great. Nice to meet you.

Exchanging Cards
Do you have a card?
Here's my card.

Response
Yes, let me get you one.
Thank you. And here's mine.

Introducing Yourself to a Receptionist
Hello. I'm Richard Carmichael of CalTrans. I'm
  here to see Georges Bernard.
Hello. I have an appointment with Georges
  Bernard. My name is Richard Carmichael.

Receptionist
I'll let Mr. Bernard know you're here.
  Please have a seat.
Hello, Mr. Carmichael. Mr. Bernard is
  expecting you. Please come this way.

Language Mastery

 1. **Matching Introductions with Business Cards:** As you listen, complete the
  missing information: company name, name, position, and phone number or
  location.

a.

ALLIED DISTRIBUTION, INC.
Alex Smith

b.
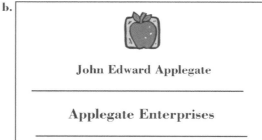
John Edward Applegate

Applegate Enterprises

c.
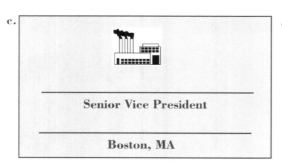
Senior Vice President

Boston, MA

d.

S & L

Director of Public Relations

Colorado Springs, CO

2. Practice the following conversations in pairs. Fill in the blanks in the last conversation before you practice it.

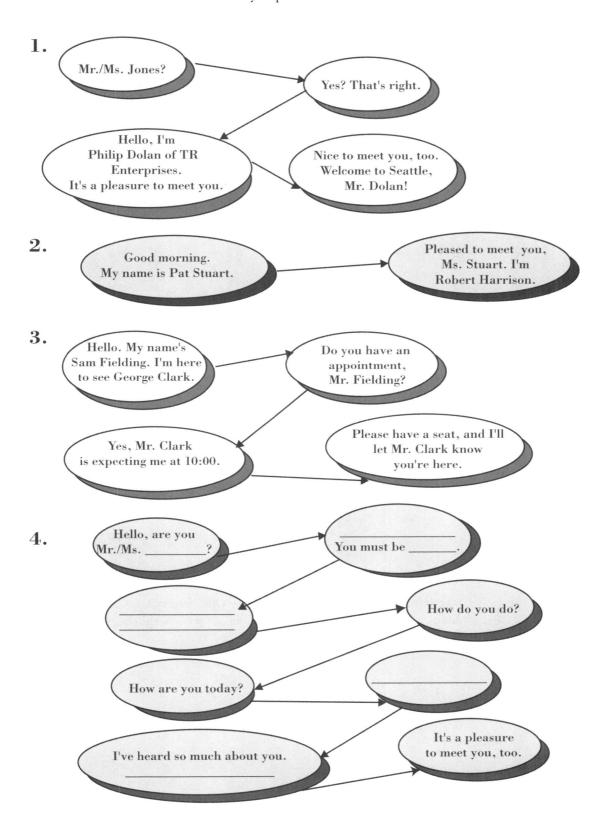

3. Listen to each item. Turn to your partner and say what would come next in the conversation. Your partner takes the next item.

   Example: How do you do?
                   How do you do? It's good to meet you.

4. **Introducing Yourself and Others:** Introduce yourself to a colleague. If possible, work with someone you don't know well.

   • Give your name and the name of your company or organization.
   • Offer your business card if you have one with you. Your colleague will do the same.
   • Ask what kind of work he or she does. After talking for a few minutes, move around the room, and introduce your colleague to someone new. Give a little information about your colleague in your introduction.
   • After they start talking, excuse yourself ("Would you excuse me?") and start again with someone new.

5. **Talking about Your Interests:**

A. Think about these ideas. Write your answers on a separate piece of paper.

   Example: something I want to do this weekend
                   I want to go swimming this weekend.

   1. somewhere I really want to visit
   2. my favorite food
   3. my favorite kind of music or musical group
   4. something I really don't care for (= I don't like at all)
   5. a person I admire
   6. my favorite film or book

B. In small groups, ask and answer questions about your ideas in A.

   Example: *A:* What do you want to do this weekend?
                   B: I really want to get out and go swimming. What do you want to do?
                   C: Well, I want to finish a report I've been working on. How about you?
                   D: I want to spend some time with my family this weekend.

C. Your instructor will collect all the papers and hand them out at random. Be sure you don't have your own paper. Read aloud what is on the paper you receive. Try to guess who wrote each paper.

Unit 3

Starting a Conversation

A. The following day, Nicole Legrand is talking with Richard Carmichael as they walk from the TVE office to a nearby restaurant for lunch. What are some possible topics of conversation in this situation?

B. Check the questions below that are not appropriate when speaking to someone from an English-speaking culture who you don't know well.

1. ❏ How old are you?
2. ❏ Where do you work?
3. ❏ Are you married?
4. ❏ Do you have children?
5. ❏ Why don't you have children?

6. ❏ What's your religion?
7. ❏ What do you do?
8. ❏ What's your salary?
9. ❏ What does your company do?
10. ❏ What's your degree in?

C. In B you checked questions that are **not OK** in English. Are any of these questions OK in the same situation in your culture? Discuss with colleagues.

Listening Practice

A. Fill in the blanks in the conversation as you listen.

Legrand: _____ , Mr. Carmichael, have you ever been to Paris before?

Carmichael: Yes, fifteen years ago as a student. _____ _____ , please call me Richard.

Legrand: Sure —_____ me Nicole. What were you studying?

Carmichael: Well, I was studying architecture. After I went back to California, I changed my major to transportation engineering.

Legrand: More practical?

Carmichael: _____ . And better employment opportunities.

Legrand: How long have you worked at CalTrans?

Carmichael: _____ , I've been there nine years now. It's interesting, and I like the people I work with. How long have you been with TVE?

B. Practice the conversation with a colleague until you can say it easily.

➤ Read each line silently. Then look at your partner when speaking.

C. This time, listen for (1) a phrase to get someone's attention, (2) a phrase to change the topic of conversation, and (3) a phrase to use while thinking of what to say.

1. Phrase to get someone's attention: _____

2. Phrase to change the topic: _____

3. Phrase to stall for time: _____

 ## Key Language

Listen, repeat, and practice aloud with a partner.

Beginning a Topic of Conversation

So, tell me, Mr. Carmichael, have you ever been to Paris before?
So, where did you learn to speak English, Ms. Legrand? Your English is really good.

Conversation Starters	**Response**
Where are you from?	I'm from New York.
What do you do (for a living)?	I'm a real estate broker.
What line of business are you in?	I'm in real estate / banking / sales.
What company do you work for?	General Motors.
What do you do for GM?	I work in the advertising department.
How long have you been with IBM?	Let's see. About four years now.
How do you like San Francisco?	It's a great city. I like it a lot.

Following up with a Question	**Response**
I was here fifteen years ago as a student.	What were you studying?
I started in French and architecture.	Oh, really?
Yes, I changed to transportation engineering.	More practical?
Right, and better employment opportunities.	How long have you been with CalTrans?

Changing the Topic	**Response**
By the way, please call me Richard.	Sure—if you'll call me Nicole.
By the way, are you free for lunch today?	That sounds great.

Language Mastery

 1. **Following the Conversation:** Listen and write the words used to start each topic of conversation. Then write your answer and a follow-up question. Finally, compare answers and practice with a colleague.

Rachel Petersen Words used to start the conversation:

_____

Your answer and follow-up:

_____

Don Baxter Words used to start the conversation:

_____

Your answer and follow-up:

_____

David Thompson Words used to start the conversation:

_____

Your answer and follow-up:

_____

 2. **Asking Follow-up Questions:** You will hear eight conversational sentences. Stop the tape after each sentence. Then turn to a colleague and ask a follow-up question.

> *Example:* It's nice to sit and relax for a moment. My boss has a lot for me to do these days.
> Really? What are you working on? Are you working on a new project?

3. **Starting Conversations:**

A. Write four general questions to start conversations.

1. _____

2. _____

3. _____

4. _____

B. In pairs, begin a conversation by asking the questions you wrote in A. Your partner will do the same. As you talk, ask follow-up questions. Then choose another partner and do the same.

4. Richard and Nicole are having dinner that evening with Jacques Dufour, TVE's production manager. Write a short conversation of 8 to 10 lines between these three people on a separate piece of paper. Then act out your conversation with colleagues.

TOEIC Tip

The Test of English for International Communication (TOEIC) is a standardized test often used to measure corporate employees' ability in English. A high TOEIC score can mean assignments abroad and promotions. TOEIC Tip sections discuss frequent questions on the TOEIC.

Tag Questions

Tag questions are a good way to start a conversation. The voice usually goes down on the tag in a tag question used as a conversation starter.

Statement	Tag Question	Expected Answer
The buffet looks great,	doesn't it?	Yes, it does.
It's nice out today,	isn't it?	Yes, beautiful.
You've worked at TVE for several years,	haven't you?	Yes, I have.
You're involved in product design,	aren't you?	Yes, I am.
You aren't traveling next week,	are you?	No, I'm not.

The TOEIC emphasizes these standard forms and many variations.

You played golf with the boss yesterday, didn't you?

It's a tough way to make a living, but someone's got to do it!

Your department got that report out, right?

Faxed it yesterday.

Your company's stock has risen a lot lately, hasn't it?

The sky's the limit.

See the Language Notes, page 173, for more explanation of tag questions.

 5. **Listening for Questions:**

A. Listen and count the questions in this everyday conversation. Count anything that functions as a question. Notice that all of these function as questions: "Did he go there?" and "He went there?" and "He went there, didn't he?"

B. How many questions did you count? _____ Check your count with the Listening Script, page 133. Practice this conversation out loud with a partner.

Unit 4

Ending a Conversation and Leave-taking

It's the second day of Richard's trip to Paris. Nicole and Richard have just had a relaxing lunch. Nicole has another appointment soon and needs to get back to the office. There is a pause in the conversation, so she says something to indicate that she needs to leave.

 Listening Practice

A. Listen and fill in the missing parts. Listen a second time to check your work.

Nicole: Well, _____ to have

a chance to talk with you in more detail. Unfortunately,

_____ to the office for a

2:00 appointment.

Richard: No problem. Let's see. I'll walk back with you—I'm going to tour the

production facility. I'm interested in seeing exactly what these trains

look like.

[Back at TVE headquarters]

Nicole: _____ , Richard. I'll

introduce you to Robert Cartier, and he'll take you over to the

production facility and show you around.

Richard: You've been so helpful. _____ all

the information you've given me. I'm looking forward to the tour.

Nicole: Yes. I hope you enjoy it. . . . Ah, Richard, let me introduce Robert

Cartier, our public relations manager. Robert, this is Richard

Carmichael from the California Department of Transportation.

Richard: How do you do, Mr. Cartier? Pleased to meet you.

Robert: How do you do, Mr. Carmichael? My pleasure.

Nicole: Richard's ready to see the production facility now. I'll see you both

tomorrow. _____ ?

Richard: Sure. See you tomorrow, Nicole. And _____ .

15

B. Practice this conversation with a colleague until you can say it easily.

➤ Read each line silently. Then look at your partner when speaking.

C. In the conversation in A, Nicole gives some conversational signals. Write the sentence she uses to say that . . .

she needs to finish the lunch meeting

_____

she needs to leave Richard and do something else

_____

she is now going to walk away from Richard and Robert

_____

 ## Key Language

Listen, repeat, and practice aloud with a partner. Which items sound informal?

Pre-Ending
I've enjoyed talking with you.

Brief Chitchat
Now don't forget to call me about that project. (*or*)
I hope you enjoy your trip to Mexico.

Ending and Leave-taking
OK. See you soon. Bye.

Pre-Endings
Well, it's been great to have a chance to talk with you. Unfortunately, I need to get back for a 2:00 appointment.
I'm afraid I have to get back to the office. I have a meeting soon. Will you excuse me?
Look at the time! I hope you'll excuse me. I need to get across town for an appointment.

Responses
I've certainly enjoyed talking to you. Let's continue our conversation later. I should get back too.
Yes, I should get going too. Thanks for all the information. I really appreciate it.
It's been great to talk to you. I hope I'll see you again soon. Let's stay in touch.

Endings
I enjoyed our lunch. I hope we'll have a chance to talk again soon.
Good-bye.
Well, I won't take any more of your time. Hope to see you soon. Good-bye.
Well, I've got to run. Talk to you soon. Bye.
I've got to get going. Take care.
Thanks. So long.

Responses
I sure hope so. It's always a pleasure to see you.
Good-bye.
It was good to talk to you. Thanks for coming by. Bye.
Sounds good. OK. See you.

You too.
Bye.

Language Mastery

 1. You are going to hear the endings of four conversations. In the blanks, write the reason for ending each conversation; then stop the tape and write what you could say next. At the end, compare responses with a colleague.

Conversation 1

Reason for ending the conversation: _____

What you would say next: _____

Conversation 2

Reason for ending the conversation: _____

What you would say next: _____

Conversation 3

Reason for ending the conversation: _____

What you would say next: _____

Conversation 4

Reason for ending the conversation: _____

What you would say next: _____

2. **Disappearing Dialog:** You have already practiced this conversation. In pairs, work with this conversation again, but this time one person looks at File 5, page 153, and the second person looks at File 9, page 156. You will see your partner's complete conversation, but part of your conversation is missing. Be ready to help if your partner forgets what to say next.

Adobe

3. **Ending Conversations:** What would you say to end conversations in these situations? Take turns with a colleague.

   a. You are at a business reception and have been talking with someone for a while. You want to end the conversation and talk to someone new.
   b. One of your clients is meeting with you to clear up some of the terms of a contract. It's been a long meeting, and you notice it's getting late.
   c. You are walking down the street with a business friend and come to the corner where you need to leave him to get back to work.
   d. You have just had a pleasant dinner with an important client. You have spent three hours with him and feel that you need to leave now.
   e. A co-worker is in your office, and you have a meeting in two minutes.

Communication Activities

1. **Conversational Round Robin:** Create a conversation with a colleague. Think of an interesting question to ask, not a question that can be answered yes or no. Answer any questions your partner has and think of ways to keep a lively conversation going. When your instructor indicates, end the conversation and begin a similar conversation with someone new.

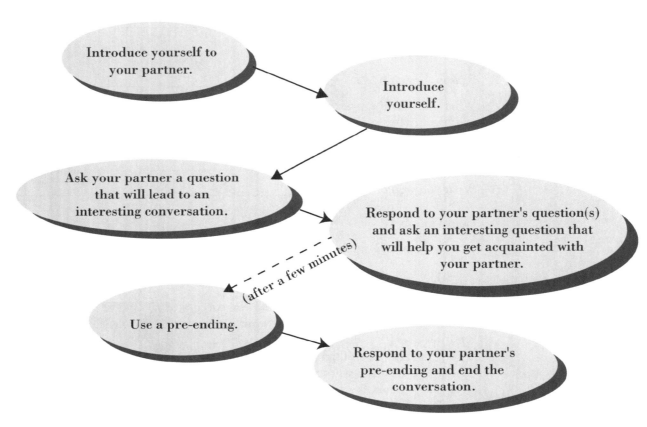

2. **Office Talk Activity:** In pairs, take turns talking briefly about each topic. When you get to a Wild Card space, talk about any topic you want.

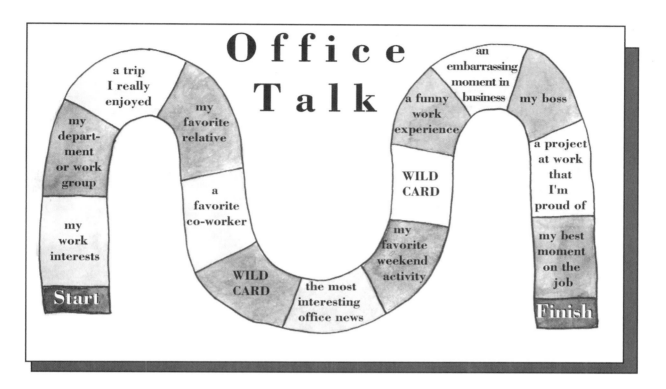

3. **Business Reception:** Plan and then give a business reception at your corporate office or language training center.

- Decide on a list of guests. (Your instructor will be able to give you some suggestions on local business people to invite.) Also decide what refreshments you will serve, where you are going to have the reception, whether or not you could have it at a local restaurant or bar, and how long the reception will last. Is an hour enough time? Is two hours too long?
- Think about layout of the room and the arrangement. Do you want to have only a few chairs so that people are encouraged to stand and mix with others?
- Make one or two people responsible for each guest. They should make introductions when the guest arrives, learn something about the guest, and be ready with several questions about that person's work.
- Everyone should also be ready to talk about themselves: why they are studying English, where they are currently employed (or hope to be employed), what their future plans are.

Following the reception, have a debriefing. Discuss these and other questions that come up.

- How did the reception go? Did you enjoy yourselves? Did your guests enjoy themselves? How do you know?
- What areas seemed to go smoothly?
- What areas do you still want to work on?
- What changes in planning would you make to improve a future reception?

Module 2

Describing Your Work

Unit 5

Talking about Facts and Figures

Susan Peterson is the manager of imports at Northwest Trading Company in Chicago. Her company is considering importing ceramic tiles from Ceramex, a leading producer of floor and wall tiles in Mexico. She will be meeting with Manuel Sanchez, manager of international sales at Ceramex. Before the meeting, Susan is reviewing economic data about Mexico.

 Listening Practice

A. Listen and write the figures you hear as Susan reviews some facts about Mexico's economy.

1. Mexico is expected to have a population of _____ million people next year.

2. This year, gross domestic product (GDP) grew at a rate of _____ percent.

3. This year, Mexico's exports amounted to U.S.$ _____ billion.

4. Imports totaled U.S.$ _____ billion, leaving a trade surplus of approximately U.S.$ _____ billion.

5. After falling to _____ last year, inflation in Mexico is expected to drop further to _____ by the end of this year.

6. The peso has appreciated modestly this year, yielding an exchange rate of around _____ to the U.S. dollar.

Exports: $106 billion

Imports: $102.7 billion

GDP: 4.3%

B. Match the expressions on the left with the best meaning on the right. Review how the expressions were used in A.

1. __ to amount to

a. The amount of money that goes out is more than what comes in.

2. __ to account for

b. to increase in value

3. __ surplus

c. to produce

4. __ deficit

d. The amount of money that comes in is more than what goes out.

5. __ to appreciate

e. to provide a satisfactory record of or an explanation for

6. __ modest

f. to equal, total

7. __ to yield

g. small in quantity, size, or value

C. Look at the graph showing Mexico's exports. Listen and check (✓) true or false for each item.

	True	False
1.	❑	❑
2.	❑	❑
3.	❑	❑
4.	❑	❑

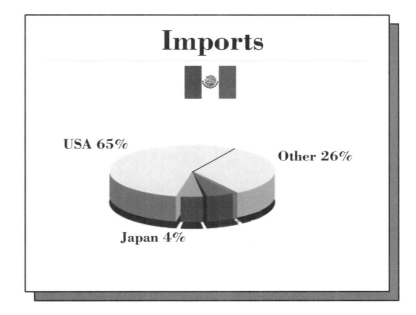

D. With a colleague, look at the graph showing Mexico's imports and answer the questions.

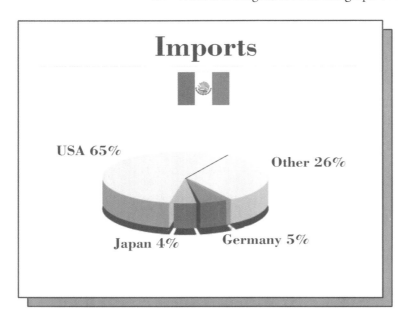

1. From which country does Mexico import the most goods?

   _____

2. After the United States, which country is the second largest importer? _____
   The third? _____

3. What percentage of imports into Mexico comes from other countries?

   _____

4. What are some of the main imports into your country? _____
   Into your colleague's country?

   _____

Facts and Figures

1. Think about times when you use facts and figures in English. If you use English to discuss any of the following at work; put a check mark next to it.

   ❑ Sales figures   ❑ Investments

   ❑ Annual revenue figures   ❑ Economic data

   ❑ Currency exchange rates   ❑ Pricing and discounts

   ❑ Percentages, decimals, fractions   ❑ Mathematical calculations

   ❑ Charts and graphs   ❑ Trends

2. Imagine that you are going to be giving a business report with a lot of facts and figures. What could you do to make sure (1) your points are clearly understood and (2) your presentation is interesting? Discuss this with a colleague.

Listening Practice

A. The following exercise will help you evaluate your listening skills related to facts and figures.

1. Write the dates you hear.

   a. _____   d. _____

   b. _____   e. _____

   c. _____   f. _____

2. Write the numbers you hear.

a. _____   d. _____

b. _____   e. _____

c. _____   f. _____

3. Write the decimals or fractions you hear.

a. _____   d. _____

b. _____   e. _____

c. _____   f. _____

B. Check the Listening Script, page 134, for the answers. Circle the ones you need to review.

 ## Key Language

Listen, repeat, and practice aloud. See also Language Notes, page 174.

Dates
We expect record sales in the year 2005 (two thousand five *or* twenty oh five).
Our company was founded on September 13, 1982 (September thirteenth, nineteen eighty-two).
By 2015, we will have been in business 50 years (two thousand fifteen *or* twenty fifteen)
B.C. = Before the birth of Christ
A.D. = Latin: *Anno Domini* (in the year since the birth of Christ)

Cardinal Numbers (quantity)	**Ordinal Numbers (dates, order, ranking)**
100 (one hundred)	1st (first)
1,000 (one thousand)	2nd (second)
1,000,000 (one million)	3rd (third)
1,000,000,000 (one billion)	13th (thirteenth)
	44th (forty-fourth)
	100th (one hundredth)

> *Notes:* *And* is used only between hundreds and tens
>   a U.S. billion = a thousand million (British)
>   a British billion = a million million (U.S.)

590 (five hundred *and* ninety)
4,796 (four thousand, seven hundred *and* ninety-six)
2,467,217 (two million, four hundred sixty-seven thousand, two hundred *and* seventeen)

Decimals, Percentages, and Fractions

44.9 (forty-four point nine)
50.97 (fifty point nine seven—numbers after decimals are spoken individually)
48% (forty-eight percent)
135% (one hundred *and* thirty-five percent)
1/4 (one-fourth)
1/3 (one-third)
1/2 (one-half)
3/4 (three-quarters)
7/8 (seven-eighths)

Language Mastery

1. A. Practice saying these dates with a partner.

1.	1861	5.	January 1, 2000	9.	1066
2.	1492	6.	October 27, 2022	10.	November 13, 1969
3.	2007	7.	258 B.C.	11.	A.D. 39
4.	February 15, 1999	8.	August 12, 1782	12.	July 29, 1905

B. Fill in the blanks with the correct preposition (*at, on, in*). Then make sentences using these expressions and dates.

1. _____ noon   3. _____ November   5. _____ 2007

2. _____ Sunday   4. _____ October 20th   6. _____ 2:00

2. Talking about Innovations

The computer (1951)

The lightbulb (1878)

The first automobile (1881)

Penicillin (discovered 1929)

The first airplane (1903)

The telephone (1876)

A. Take turns asking and answering questions about these innovations.

Example: Do you know when the first car was invented?
Yes, the first car was invented in 1881.

B. Now with a colleague, make a list of the ten most important inventions (in your opinion) to come to market over the past fifty years. Give the approximate year (or decade) that each product appeared on the market. Discuss how these inventions have changed people's lives.

 3. Listen and circle the number you hear. Then practice saying these numbers with a colleague.

1. a. 50   b. 15   c. 55
2. a. 18,000   b. 88,000   c. 80,000
3. a. 33   b. 30   c. 13
4. a. 214   b. 240   c. 204
5. a. 543   b. 533   c. 554
6. a. 3,221   b. 3,021   c. 3,321
7. a. 4,798,321   b. 4,978,321   c. 4,798,301

 4. Listen and fill in the blanks. Then practice saying these figures with a partner.

Thursday, November 13

Dow Jones Industrial Average
Closed at: _____

The NASDAQ Composite
Closed at: _____

Standard & Poor's 500
Closed at: _____

↗ _____   ↗ _____   ↗ _____

_____   _____   _____
IBM _____ General Electric _____ Microsoft _____ Exxon _____ GM _____

5. Look at the examples of the following graphs. Why might you choose one kind of graph over another to best represent your data?

PIE GRAPH

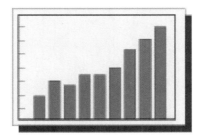

BAR GRAPH

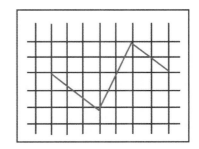

LINE GRAPH

6. **Research Activity:** Use the Internet or a library to find population figures for Mexico, South Korea, Brazil, India, Indonesia, Russia, the United States, and Japan. Finish the bar graph to reflect the population figures. Then with a colleague, discuss each one's ranking worldwide.

Example: China has 2.8 billion people. It ranks first worldwide in terms of population.

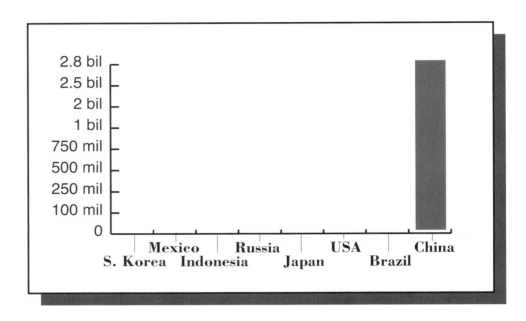

Unit 6

Introducing Your Company

Manuel Sanchez from Ceramex is in Chicago to discuss exporting ceramic tiles from Mexico to the United States. In his meeting with Susan Peterson of Northwest Trading Company, he is presenting information about his company.

ceramic: made of baked clay

 Listening Practice

A. Listen as you look at the illustrations. Then practice introducing Ceramex to a partner.

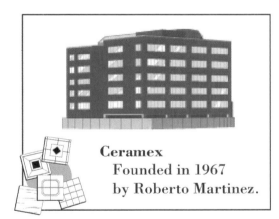

Ceramex
Founded in 1967
by Roberto Martinez.

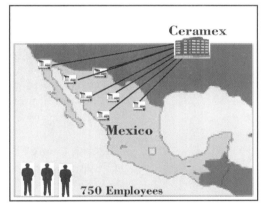

Ceramex

Mexico

750 Employees

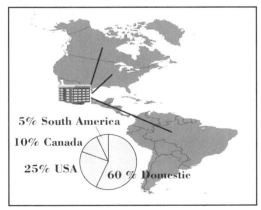

5% South America
10% Canada
25% USA
60 % Domestic

B. Write five questions about Ceramex using the following question words. Then practice asking and answering the questions with a partner.

> *Example:*   When was Ceramex founded?
> Ceramex was founded in 1967.

1. Who _____ ?

2. Where _____ ?

3. What _____ ?

4. How many _____ ?

5. What percentage _____ ?

 ## Key Language

Listen, repeat, and practice aloud.

Providing Company History
Ceramex was founded in 1967.
Procter & Gamble was established in 1837 by William Procter and James Gamble.
The company has been expanding gradually since 1982.

Describing Main Products or Services
Ceramex produces floor and ceiling tiles.
Lucent Technologies develops and manufactures communication systems.

Clarifying Company Activities
What kind of tiles does your company produce?
Exactly what type of systems does Lucent Technologies develop?

Talking about Reputation
Ceramex is recognized as one of the leading producers of floor and ceiling tiles
    in the world.
Lucent Technologies is a world leader in the design and development of
    communication systems.

Describing Location, Workforce, and Revenue
Ceramex has seven factories in northern Mexico.
Lucent Technologies' headquarters are in New Jersey. It has offices, subsidiaries,
    or distributors in more than 90 countries.
Ceramex employs 750 people in Mexico.
Lucent Technologies has 121,000 employees worldwide with approximately
    82 percent in the United States.
Lucent Technologies' total revenue for fiscal year 1996 was $23.3 billion.
In 1997, Ceramex reported annual sales of $200 million.

Language Mastery

1. Complete the following sentences. Then take turns describing your company or organization to a partner.

    a. My company (or organization) was founded in _____ .

    b. It produces / manufactures / provides _____ .

    c. It is recognized as _____ .

    d. Its headquarters are located in _____ .

    e. It employs _____ .

    f. Revenues for last year were_____ .

2. **Exchanging Company Information:** Work with a colleague. One person looks at File 3, page 152, and the other at File 8, page 155. Each of you will have information about an international company. Take turns asking and answering questions on the basis of this information.

3. A. The following milestones provide a history of the Sony Corporation, 1946–97. Put the milestones in the correct order; numbering 1 through 8.

    ___ After the tape recorder came transistors: Morita and Ibuka bought the technology from Western Electric and turned it into a pocket-size radio in 1957.

    ___ The Walkman portable cassette player was introduced in 1979 and came from Morita's recognition that "young people cannot live without music."

    _1_ In 1946, Akio Morita and Ibuka Masaru started a manufacturing business on the third floor of a bombed-out Tokyo department store. First named Tokyo Telecommunications Engineering Corporation, the company was later named Sony.

    ___ In 1997, Sony's annual sales were $45.67 billion, and the company employed 163,000 people worldwide.

    ___ After the Walkman came other major innovations including the CD player in 1982, the 8mm video camera in 1985, the 36-inch HD Trinitron TV in 1990, and a digital video camera in 1993.

    ___ The company's first products were a rice cooker and then a reel-to-reel tape recorder.

    ___ In recognition of his global achievements, Queen Elizabeth awarded Akio Morita an honorary knighthood in 1992. In 1993, he resigned as chairman of Sony.

    ___ In 1960, Sony produced the world's first transistor TV.

    B.   Building a Company History

    Sit in a circle in groups of 4 to 8. Each person will select one of Sony's milestones. Study the milestone for a few minutes so that you can say it perfectly. The first person will begin and state the first major milestone. The second person will listen, paraphrase the first person's sentence, and then add his or her own milestone. This should continue until Sony's story has been told.

    Example: (paraphrase) In 1946, Akio Morita and Ibuka Masaru founded Tokyo Telecommunications Engineering Corporation. The company name was later changed to Sony.

TOEIC Tip

Passive Voice
The use of the passive voice is common in business when

1. the emphasis is placed on the object receiving the action;

   Ceramex was founded in 1967. / Roberto was promoted last week.

2. the doer of the action (by phrase) is people in general or the doer is unknown or unimportant;

   Ceramex is recognized as one of the leading tile producers in the world.

3. the emphasis is on the process.

   Raw materials are purchased and delivered to the Production Department.

Form: *be* + Past Participle. Notice the forms of *be* in these examples:

Active	**Passive**
John Phillips founded Tile Works.	Tile Works was founded by John Phillips.
The director will promote her next week.	She will be promoted next week.
People recognize him as a genius.	He is recognized as a genius.
Employees must turn in time sheets by 5:00.	Time sheets must be turned in by 5:00.
Someone has developed the procedures.	The procedures have been developed.

Refer to Language Notes, page 178, for more help with the passive voice.

4. With a colleague, make the following statements passive.

   a. Researchers are developing new products every day.

      _____

   b. After the products leave the manufacturing plant, someone sends them to the distributor.

      _____

   c. People recognize Microsoft as one of the leading software companies in the world.

      _____

   d. The company sold more than 10,000 units last year.

      _____

   e. The company will build a new factory next year.

      _____

f.   The company has paid employees according to their performance rather than seniority.

_____

g.   Someone is going to announce the merger of PCI and World Technology next week.

_____

h.   You can return the product if it is defective.

_____

i.   Someone has made a mistake.

_____

j.   The company will give bonuses at the end of the year if there is a profit.

_____

5. **Describing Your Company:** Prepare a short description of your company or organization. Present it to your partner or in small groups. Be sure to include the following information.

   •   When the company was founded and a brief history
   •   Main products or services
   •   Location of headquarters, manufacturing facilities, branch offices
   •   Number of employees
   •   Annual sales

Unit 7

Describing Company Organization

Manuel Sanchez is describing the organizational structure of Ceramex to Susan Peterson at Northwest Trading Company.

Listening Practice

A. Listen and then fill in the organizational chart.

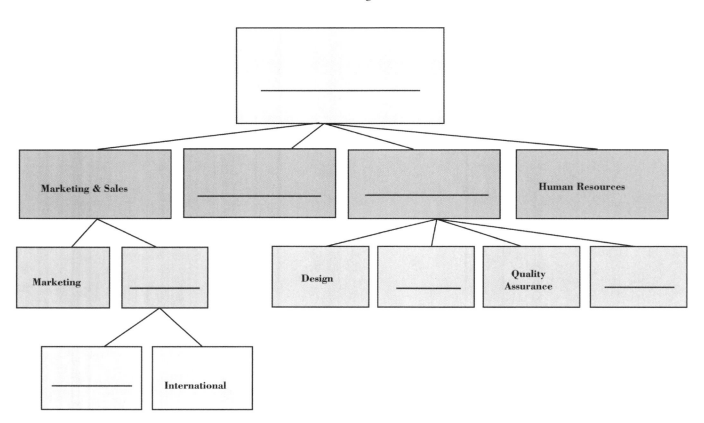

B. Write three questions about the organizational structure of Ceramex. Then ask a partner these questions.

Example: How is the Sales Department divided?

It's divided into domestic and international sales.

1. _____?
2. _____?
3. _____?

⊙⊙ Key Language

Listen, repeat, and practice aloud with a partner.

Describing Company Organization　　**Response**
How is your company structured?　　Ceramex is divided into four main divisions.
Tell me about your company's organization.　　Our company is organized around functional
　　groups and project teams.

Talking about Lines of Authority
The chief executive officer (CEO) is in charge of the overall direction of the company.
The chief financial officer reports to the CEO.
The vice president of production is responsible for product design, manufacturing, and quality.

Describing Departments
Production is divided into four sections.
The Sales Department is further divided into domestic and international sales.
The Procurement Department is responsible for purchasing raw materials and production
　supplies.

Language Mastery

1. **Describing Department Functions:** The illustration gives examples of typical
   departments in corporations. With a colleague, discuss what the people in these
   departments do. Does your company or organization have similar departments?

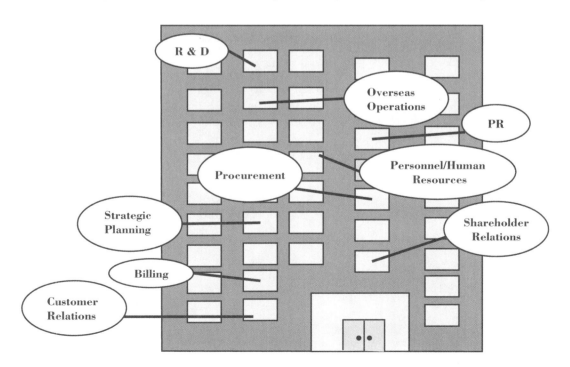

2. Listen and then write the titles of the following people in a U.S. company.

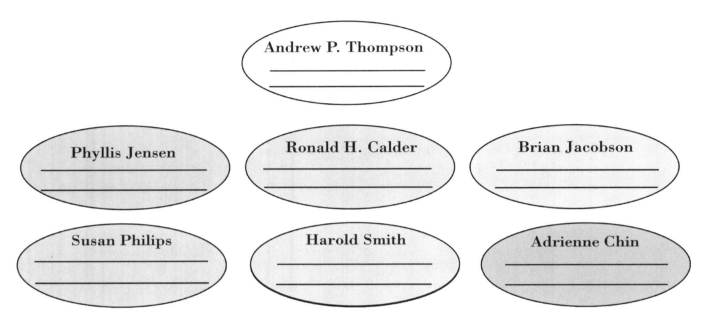

3. **Understanding U.S. Titles:** The following are common titles in U.S. corporations.

   A. Put the titles in order from highest (1) to lowest (7) rank.

   ___ assistant general manager

   ___ manager

   ___ chair of the board

   ___ executive vice president and chief operating officer

   ___ president and chief executive officer

   ___ general manager

   ___ assistant manager

   B. With a colleague, compare these titles to those in your company.

4. **Talking about Lines of Authority:** Refer to exercise 3 and ask a partner about the lines of authority.

   Example: *A:* Whom does the CEO report to?
                B: He reports to the chair of the board.

5. Draw a blank organizational chart of your company or organization (or a department in your company) and give it to a partner. Each of you should present your company's organizational structure, explaining lines of authority and department function. Repeat information as necessary. Check to make sure your partner filled out the chart correctly. Be ready to ask your partner three questions about his or her organization.

Unit 8

Describing Job Responsibilities

Susan Peterson asks Manuel Sanchez about his job responsibilities at Ceramex.

🔘 Listening Practice

A. Listen and check (✓) true or false for each statement. If the sentence is false, change it to make it true.

	True	False
1. Manuel has been at Ceramex for seven years.	❑	❑
2. He is now in marketing and sales.	❑	❑
3. He supervises a staff of twenty people.	❑	❑
4. He travels about 80 percent of the time for his job.	❑	❑

B. Now listen again and then discuss these questions.

1. What is Manuel responsible for?
2. What do you think is involved in heading the international marketing and sales department at Ceramex?

Key Language

Listen, repeat, and practice aloud with a partner.

Asking about Job Responsibilities	Response
What are you responsible for at Ceramex?	I'm responsible for coordinating international sales and marketing efforts.
	I'm in charge of the microprocessor products group.
What exactly do you do at P&G?	I oversee all international sales and marketing activities.
	I supervise a staff of 150 people.
What does Helen do?	She heads the PR Department and handles all international correspondence.
What is the most challenging part of your job?	I have to deal with customer complaints all day.

❖   What parts of speech can follow *be responsible for* and *be in charge of?*

Describing a Typical Day
Well, I usually get to the office around 7:30 in the morning.
I often begin by going through my in basket.
After I open my mail, I prioritize my activities for the day.

❖   What verb tense is used to describe typical activities?

See Language Notes, page 180, to review verb tenses.

Language Mastery

 1. Listen and write what the following people are responsible for.

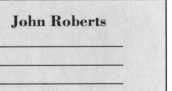

John Roberts

_____
_____

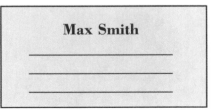

Max Smith

_____
_____

Sara Burton

_____
_____

2. Complete the following sentences with your own ideas using tasks and responsibilities you are familiar with.

    a. John is responsible for _____ .

    b. Nancy handles _____ .

    c. Susan heads _____ .

    d. Alex reports _____ .

    e. Laura deals _____ .

    f. Jack supervises _____ .

    g. Richard oversees_____ .

    h. Peter Thomas is in charge _____ .

3. **Talking about Job Responsibilities:** Ask a colleague these questions.

    a. What are you responsible for at your company or organization?

    b. Who do you report to? What is his or her title?

    c. What do you organize or supervise at work? Who reports to you?

    d. What are you in charge of (project, activity, team, department)?

    e. What problems do you typically have to deal with?

 4. A. Listen as Manuel talks about a typical day at work. Then look at the illustrations and take turns retelling his story with a colleague.

B. Describe your typical day at work to a colleague. What are your main activities?

Professional Protocol

Global Cultures

1. Think about business presentations in your country. Which of the following apply?

    - ❏ Eye contact with the audience is important.
    - ❏ Reading a speech from a printed text is common.
    - ❏ The speaker follows a clear outline with logical steps.
    - ❏ Computerized, four-color visual aids are common.
    - ❏ Humor, jokes, and funny stories are used frequently.
    - ❏ Handouts are usually given to the audience.
    - ❏ The speaker gets to the point directly.
    - ❏ It is common to apologize for something at the beginning of the presentation (poor language skills, lack of preparation, etc.).
    - ❏ The audience asks a lot of questions.
    - ❏ The speaker stands in one place while giving the presentation.

2. Describe a typical business presentation in your country to a colleague.

Guidelines for Presentations in the United States

A U.S. audience will have certain expectations about business presentations they hear. The following points are important for a U.S. audience.

- When presenting company information, think about your audience. What are they most interested in? Tailor your presentation to their specific interests.
- Remember the **three-week rule:** People will forget almost everything you tell them, so identify three or four points that you want them to remember three weeks later. Emphasize these points.
- Begin with a very short introduction, for example: "I'd like to give you some background information about Ceramex." After a few background sentences, go right into the "meat" of your presentation. North Americans tend to get impatient with long introductions.

- Work from an outline or write down your main points rather than whole sentences. This will help organize your presentation, and it will keep you from reading your notes.
- Add one or two human interest points, for example, a personal anecdote or a story about the founder of the company.
- Remember to keep your presentation short and to the point. Practice out loud so that you can keep to the time allotted for your presentation.
- Use high-quality graphics for your presentation, if possible four-color computerized graphics or clear, bold text on overhead transparencies or slides. Use your visuals to reinforce main points and important facts and figures.
- When presenting quantitative information, remember to be selective. Don't overwhelm your audience with too many facts and figures. Pronounce numbers clearly.
- Practice, practice, practice. Experts recommend practicing your presentation three times using your visuals. If you don't practice enough, your presentation may not be polished. On the other hand, if you practice too much, you may sound like a robot.

Communication Activities

1. **Company Presentation:** Give a five-minute oral presentation about your company organization. Be sure to include some of the following.

   - When the company was founded
   - Main products or services
   - Location of headquarters, manufacturing facilities, branch offices
   - Number of employees
   - Organizational structure
   - Departments
   - Annual sales
   - Major customers
   - Main competitors
   - Competitive strengths

2. **Country Presentation:** Give a five-minute oral presentation about the economy of your country. Use the Internet or a library to find the most up-to-date information. Be sure to include some of the following.

   - Profile of the country's economy
   - Rate of growth per year
   - Economic strengths
   - Economic weaknesses
   - Leading exports
   - Leading imports
   - Leading trading partners
   - Gross domestic product
   - World gross national product (GNP) ranking
   - GNP per capita
   - Inflation
   - Unemployment rate
   - Other economic performance indicators

3. **Cartoon:** With a colleague, discuss the cartoon and answer the questions.

a. Take turns explaining what happens in each frame of the cartoon.
b. What is the main point of the cartoon?
c. Which departments are mentioned in this company?

_____ _____ _____

_____ _____ _____

_____ _____ _____

_____

d. Based on the departments mentioned, what kind of company do you think this is?
e. Write all of the negative terms that are used to describe people.

_____ _____ _____

_____ _____ _____

_____ _____ _____

_____

f. Ask a native speaker what the terms mean and which ones are used commonly today. Would you really expect to hear these terms used in companies?

Module 3

Telephoning

Unit 9

Problems Telephoning

Jack Lee is in charge of purchasing at Global Telecom in San Francisco, California, where he buys parts for telecommunications equipment. He has been trying to telephone one of his suppliers but has been having problems.

Photo Credit: Tom McCarthy. Copyright © 1996 The Stock Solution

Listening Practice

A. Listen as Jack tells his assistant the problems he's been having. What does he complain about?

B. Listen again and check (✓) true or false for each statement. If the sentence is false, correct it to make it true.

		True	False
1.	He tried to call Peter Miller at MCI.	❑	❑
2.	The first four times he called, the line was busy.	❑	❑
3.	When he got through, the receptionist put him on hold.	❑	❑
4.	He was on hold for two or three minutes.	❑	❑
5.	When he called the second time he was able to speak to Peter Miller.	❑	❑
6.	Jack is considering using another supplier.	❑	❑

C. With a colleague, discuss these questions.

1. How long is it acceptable to put someone on hold?
2. Why, in your opinion, did these problems occur?
3. How serious are the problems Jack Lee experienced? Why?

D. Look at the following cartoon with a colleague. Describe the problem and the attitude of the two people in the cartoon.

"Mr. Lee called to say that he's fed up with leaving messages. Oh, and he also called 32 times this week."

E. The expressions on the left were used in the conversation in A. Match them with the best meaning on the right. Write the letters in the blanks.

1. __ The line was busy.   a. to be cut off

2. __ to get through   b. Someone was using the phone.

3. __ to hang up   c. to send the call to another person

4. __ to transfer the call   d. to put the receiver down in order

                                    to end the call

5. __ to be disconnected   e. to get connected to

> *Note: Phone* can be used as a *verb* (I'm going to phone him tonight) or as a *noun* (I need to use the phone).

Telephone Skills

Discuss these questions in groups.

1. What kind of calls do you make in English?

2. What is difficult about talking on the phone in English?

  ❏ Getting through to the right person?

  ❏ Starting a conversation?

  ❏ Organizing your thoughts?

  ❏ Understanding the other person?

  ❏ Making sure you are understood?

3. What are two suggestions for making telephoning in English easier?

Professional Protocol

Global Cultures

1. What are two or three important rules of telephone etiquette in your country?
2. In your culture, are certain behaviors considered rude when telephoning?

Guidelines for Making Telephone Calls in English

- Think about your call before you make it. Write a few notes so that you can remember the main points you want to make. Practice any difficult expressions before making the call.
- State your purpose for calling clearly. Speak slowly and clearly, especially when you give your name.
- Answer incoming calls quickly and always return calls within 24 hours.
- Listen for key words and try to understand the general meaning. Don't try to understand every word.
- Don't listen silently. Respond to what the other person is saying, even if just to say, "Really?" "I know what you mean," "Is that right?" "That's interesting," "Oh, I see." This will make your end of the conversation more active and responsive.
- If you don't understand something, ask the person to repeat what he or she said: "Excuse me, would you mind repeating that?" "Could you please repeat that?" or just "Excuse me?"
- Always confirm important dates, times, and phone numbers. You could say, "Let me make a note of this. Our appointment is at two o'clock next Wednesday, right?"
- End your conversations on a friendly note; for example, "It was nice talking to you," "I appreciate the chance to discuss this with you," "I'm glad we had a chance to talk about this."
- Avoid calling someone at home about business unless it is urgent. When calling someone at home, avoid dinnertime and try to call before 9:00 P.M. Begin with "I'm sorry to bother you at home, but . . ."

Unit 10

Making a Phone Call

Sung-Wook Jung is the North American sales manager for SRG Electronics, a Korean company that produces parts for telecommunications equipment. Mr. Jung is making a cold call to Jack Lee.

cold call: a call to someone you don't know, usually for a sales purpose

🔳 Listening Practice

A. Listen to the conversation and answer these questions.

1. Who answers the telephone at Global Telecom?
2. What reason does Mr. Jung give for calling?

B. Listen again and then fill in the blanks.

Receptionist:	Good morning, Global Telecom.
	_____ ?
Jung:	Good morning. I'd _____
	Jack Lee in purchasing, please.
Receptionist:	May I _____ ?
Jung:	Yes, _____ Sung-Wook
	Jung of SRG Electronics in Korea. I'm calling to talk about our
	telecommunications equipment.
Receptionist:	One moment and _____
	your call.

C. Practice that conversation with a colleague until you can say it easily.

➤ Read each line silently. Then look at your partner when speaking.

Key Language

Listen, repeat, and practice aloud with a partner.

Answering the Phone
Good morning, General Electric. May I help you?
Good afternoon, Sunlight Electronics. How may
    I direct your call?

Response
Yes. May I please speak to Max Evans?
I'd like to speak to someone in billing,
    please.

Asking to Speak to Someone
May I please speak to Susan Evans?
I'd like to speak to Mark Brown, please.
Is Alexandra in? (business informal)
Is Tom there? (home informal)

Response
This is Susan.
Just a moment, please.
Speaking.
This is Tom.

Asking Who Is Calling
May I say who's calling?
Who's calling, please?

Response
Yes, this is Sandra Peterson from IBM.
My name is Sung-Wook Jung. I'm
    with SRG Electronics.

Stating the Purpose of the Call
I'm returning Mr. Smith's phone call.
I'm calling to set up an appointment with Mr. Lee.

Response
Thank you. I'll connect you.
OK, please hold while I transfer you.

Taking Messages
Mr. Johnson is out of the office at the moment.
    Would you like to leave a message?
Ms. Perkins is in a meeting. Could I take a
    message?
How do you spell your last name?

Response
Yes, please have him call Elizabeth
    Brown at 493- 2591.
Yes, please ask her to return my call. /
    No, thanks. I'll call back later.
It's W-I-N-S-T-O-N. Tom Winston.

Language Mastery

1. Ask a colleague to do the following.

    a. Answer the phone at your company or organization.
    b. Ask to speak to Elizabeth Jordan.
    c. Ask for the caller's name.
    d. Give your name and company name.
    e. You are calling to get a current price list. State the purpose of the call.
    f. Allison Adams, your office mate, is at lunch. Tell the caller that Allison is at
       lunch and offer to take a message.
    g. Ask a colleague how to spell his or her name.

2. **Understanding Phone Numbers:** Write the telephone numbers you hear. Then practice the numbers aloud.

> *Note:* Remember to say each number separately. For example, for the number (213) 569-2108, say, "Area code two one three (pause), five six nine (pause), two one oh eight."

a. _____   d. _____

b. _____   e. _____

c. _____   f. _____

 3. **Listening for Key Words:** Key words communicate the main points. Listen to the following telephone messages. Underline the key words you hear. Then compare answers with a partner.

Example: "Good morning, Mr. Lee. This is <u>Judith Taylor</u> of <u>Microproducts</u>. I'm calling to confirm your <u>meeting</u> with <u>Peter Miller</u> on <u>Friday</u> at <u>10:00</u>. Please call if there's a <u>problem</u> with this time."

a. "Hello, John. This is Irene Jenkins. I'm calling to remind you of our appointment next Tuesday at 2:30. I'll see you then."

b. "Hi. This is Tracy. Sorry I'm late. I got stuck in rush hour traffic. I should be there in about 30 minutes. See you."

 4. **Taking Phone Messages:** Fill in the chart as you listen to three conversations. Write the name of the caller, his or her company or organization, and the person being called.

	Caller	Company or Organization	Person Called
Call 1			
Call 2			
Call 3			

5. Listen to the next two calls and take a message for each.

➤ Listen for key words.

a.

To _____
WHILE YOU WERE OUT
M _____
of _____
Phone (_____)_____
Telephoned ☐　Please Call ☐
Will call again ☐　Returned Your Call ☐
Urgent ☐　Called to See You ☐
MESSAGE: _____
_____
_____
_____

b.

To _____
WHILE YOU WERE OUT
M _____
of _____
Phone (_____)_____
Telephoned ☐　Please Call ☐
Will call again ☐　Returned Your Call ☐
Urgent ☐　Called to See You ☐
MESSAGE: _____
_____
_____
_____

6. Practice the following conversation with a colleague.

　　A:　　Good morning. **Network Exchange.** May I help you?
　　B:　　Good morning. I'd like to speak to **Patricia Anderson,** please.
　　A:　　I'm sorry, **she's in a meeting at the moment.** Would you like to leave a message?
　　B:　　Yes. Please ask **her** to call Robert Sonntag at 565-1254.
　　A:　　OK, Mr. Sonntag, I'll give **her** the message.

Now, practice making similar calls by replacing the boldfaced words with the information presented in each of the following scenarios. For the last scenario, discuss what "out to lunch" means.

Universal Insurance **Tom Johnson** Out of town this week	**Creative Computer Systems** **Roberta Allen** Away from her desk	**FRG Engineering** **Ralph Langstrom** At lunch until 1:30
Secret Haven Resorts **Susan Sutherland** In a meeting	**Italia Designs** **Frederico Antonioni** On another line	I'm afraid he's out to lunch!

7. With a partner, describe what the following items are used for.

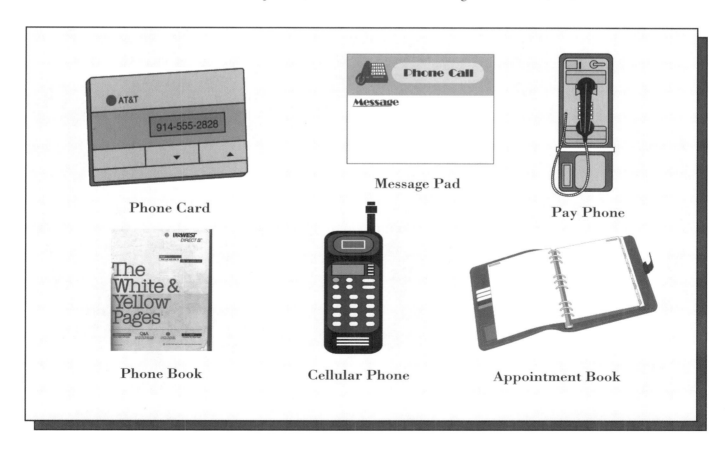

Phone Card

Message Pad

Pay Phone

Phone Book

Cellular Phone

Appointment Book

Unit 11

Scheduling a Meeting

The receptionist has just told Jack Lee of Global Telecom that Mr. Jung of SRG Electronics in Korea is on the phone.

 Listening Practice

A. Listen to the conversation. Which of the following do you think are probably Mr. Jung's objectives for this initial sales phone call?

❏ Introduce himself and his company

❏ Find out who Global Telecom's suppliers are

❏ Describe his products in detail

❏ Set up a meeting

❏ Establish a relationship

❏ Discuss prices

B. Practice this conversation with a colleague until you can say it easily.

➤ Read each line silently. Then look at your partner when speaking.

Lee: Hello, Mr. Jung. Jack Lee speaking.

Jung: Hello, Mr. Lee. I'm with SRG Electronics. I was hoping to talk to you about our line of electronic parts.

Lee: Oh, yes, I've heard of SRG. How are things going in Korea?

Jung: Good, thanks. In fact, recently there's been a lot of demand for our parts, so we've been very busy.

Lee: Glad to hear that. I'd certainly be interested in your prices.

Jung: Well, it just so happens I'm going to be in San Francisco next week. I was wondering if you'd have time to get together.

Lee: You bet. When will you be here?

Jung: Next Wednesday and Thursday. What does your schedule look like?

Lee: Um . . . Let me check my calendar. (after a few moments) Let's see, I have a meeting on Wednesday morning. How about Wednesday afternoon at about two o'clock?

Jung: Two o'clock is fine.

it just so happens: by chance
to get together: to meet, to spend time together

C. Look at the following cartoon with a partner. What point is being made? How are assignments usually communicated to you in your company?

DILBERT by Scott Adams

PRIORITIZING YOUR WORK

 Key Language

Listen, repeat, and practice aloud with a partner.

Stating Your Business Activity
SRG specializes in electronic parts for telecommunications equipment.
Star Computers develops business applications software.
Our company is involved in retail banking.

Setting up a Meeting or an Appointment
I'll be in San Francisco next week, and I'd like to set up a meeting.
I'd like to schedule a meeting to show you some of our products.

Response
That's a great idea. When will you be here?
Sure. I'd like to hear more about your products.

Finding a Suitable Time	**Response**
I'll be in town on Wednesday and Thursday. Do you have time to meet then?	Yes, I'm free Wednesday afternoon.
Shall we set up a time?	Sure. Let me check my calendar.
Are you free on Wednesday morning?	Let's see. I have a meeting then. What about in the afternoon?
Is two o'clock convenient for you?	Yes, two o'clock is fine. / I'm sorry, but I have another appointment then.
Let's make it Wednesday at two o'clock then.	That's fine with me.

Asking Where to Meet	**Suggesting Options**
Where would you like to meet?	How about at my office?
Where shall we meet?	Why don't we meet at your office?

Language Mastery

 1. **Listening for Stressed Words:** Remember that listening for stressed words will help your comprehension on the phone. Listen to the following messages left on answering machines. Underline the stressed words you hear. Then look at the words you underlined. Do the underlined words communicate the main point?

Example: "Good <u>afternoon</u>, <u>Jack</u>. This is <u>Helen Smith</u> with <u>Sprint</u>. Please give me a <u>call</u> at your <u>earliest convenience</u>. My number is <u>(307) 449-6767</u>."

   a. "Good morning, Dorothy. This is Claudia Bransford. I'm afraid I have to cancel our meeting today. My daughter is sick with the flu. I'll give you a call in a few days to reschedule. I'm terribly sorry about this."

   b. "Hello, Jim. This is Bill Sherman at Merrill Lynch. Give me a call as soon as possible. I've got some news about a stock offering. My number is 483-8000."

 2. **Arranging Appointments:** Susan Potter, Jack Lee's assistant at Global Telecom, receives two calls this morning. Listen and then write the name of the person who called, the time, the date, and the location of the appointment.

	Person	Time & Date	Location
Call 1			
Call 2			

3. **Language Review:** With a colleague, take turns asking these questions. Begin with "How would you . . . ?"

   a. . . . answer the phone for your company?
   b. . . . ask to speak to Yuko Tanaka?
   c. . . . ask for the caller's name?
   d. . . . give your name and company (or organization) when calling someone?
   e. . . . state the purpose of your call?
   f. . . . state your company's business activity?
   g. . . . suggest setting up a meeting?
   h. . . . offer to take a message?
   i. . . . ask when Ms. Black will be back in the office?
   j. . . . ask about a convenient time to reach Mr. Thompson?
   k. . . . ask if Wednesday is a convenient time for a meeting?
   l. . . . ask if the caller would like to leave a message for Ms. Jackson?

4. **Scheduling an Appointment:** Role-play the following conversation with a colleague. One of you will be Peter Miller and the other Jack Lee. Follow this sequence.

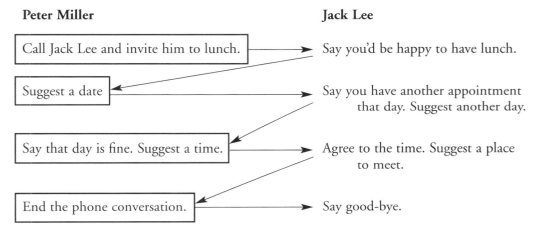

Peter Miller

Call Jack Lee and invite him to lunch.

Suggest a date

Say that day is fine. Suggest a time.

End the phone conversation.

Jack Lee

Say you'd be happy to have lunch.

Say you have another appointment that day. Suggest another day.

Agree to the time. Suggest a place to meet.

Say good-bye.

TOEIC Tip

Identifying Logical Answers

Understanding colloquial language is one of the most difficult parts of telephoning. The TOEIC exam includes a listening section with commonly asked questions. The key to answering correctly is to focus on the main idea of the question and choose the best answer. The other choices may restate key words you hear and confuse you, but don't forget the point of the original question.

   Example: You will hear: "How's it going?" The choices are
   _A:_ I'm going to lunch, thanks.
   _B:_ Good! How about you?
   _C:_ Yes, I'd like to go with you.

The correct answer is B. When someone asks, "How's it going?" he or she wants to know how you are doing.

5. **Identifying Logical Answers:** You will hear a question followed by three responses. The question and the responses will be spoken just one time. You are to choose the best response to each question by circling A, B, or C. After you finish, check your answers in the Listening Script and then listen again.

1. A   B   C

2. A   B   C

3. A   B   C

4. A   B   C

5. A   B   C

6. A   B   C

7. A   B   C

8. A   B   C

Unit 12

Ending a Phone Conversation

After arranging a time for a meeting, Mr. Jung and Mr. Lee end their telephone conversation.

Listening Practice

A. Listen and check (✓) true or false for each statement. If the sentence is false, change it to make it true.

	True	False
1. They decide to meet at Mr. Lee's office.	❏	❏
2. Mr. Lee's office is on Sutter Street.	❏	❏
3. Mr. Jung is staying at the Marriott Hotel.	❏	❏
4. The appointment is for next Thursday.	❏	❏
5. Mr. Lee's office is six blocks from Mr. Jung's hotel.	❏	❏

B. Listen again, and then fill in the details of the upcoming meeting:

From The Desk Of
Jung Sung-Wook

Meeting Notes

Meeting with: _____

Company: _____

Day & Time: _____

Location: _____

Address: _____

Directions: _____

C. Mr. Jung usually writes a letter to confirm information communicated on the phone. Complete the following letter with the necessary information. Then compare your letter with a colleague's.

SRG Electronics
140-013 Sungji Bldg.
40-712, 3-Ga Hangang-Ro,
Yongsan-Ku, Seoul, Korea
Tel: 82 2 220-7331, Fax 82 2 220-0781

July 14, _____

Mr. Jack Lee
Purchasing Manager
Global Telecom
555 California Street
San Francisco, CA 94110, USA

Dear Mr. Lee:

I enjoyed speaking with you on the phone today. I wanted to write to confirm our appointment next week.

_____

_____

_____

_____

I'm looking forward to meeting with you. Give me a call if you have any questions.

Sincerely,

Jung Sung-Wook

Jung Sung-Wook
Sales Manager, North America

Encl. SRG Electronics brochure

Key Language

Listen, repeat, and practice aloud with a partner.

Confirming Information	**Response**
OK, so our appointment is for next Wednesday at two o'clock?	That's right.
So that's next Thursday at three o'clock?	Exactly.

Asking for Repetition	**Response**
I'm sorry, could you repeat that?	Certainly. / Sure.
Would you mind repeating that?	Not at all. (= It is not a problem.)

Preclosing (signaling the closing)	**Response**
Well, I'm glad I had a chance to talk with you.	I've enjoyed talking with you, too.
Well, I've got to get going. Let's talk more about this next week.	OK, I'll give you a call next week. Good talking to you.

Closing	**Response**
I'm looking forward to our meeting next Wednesday.	Yes and I'm looking forward to hearing about your new products.
I'll see you next week. Good-bye.	Good-bye.

Language Mastery

 1. **Ending Phone Calls:** You will hear the endings of three phone conversations. Write the reason that is used to end the conversation. Then write what you would say next.

	What reason is used to end the conversation?	**What would you say next?**
a		
b		
c		

2. **Conversation Activity:** In pairs, practice the conversation activity using language from the module. Then change roles and try it again.

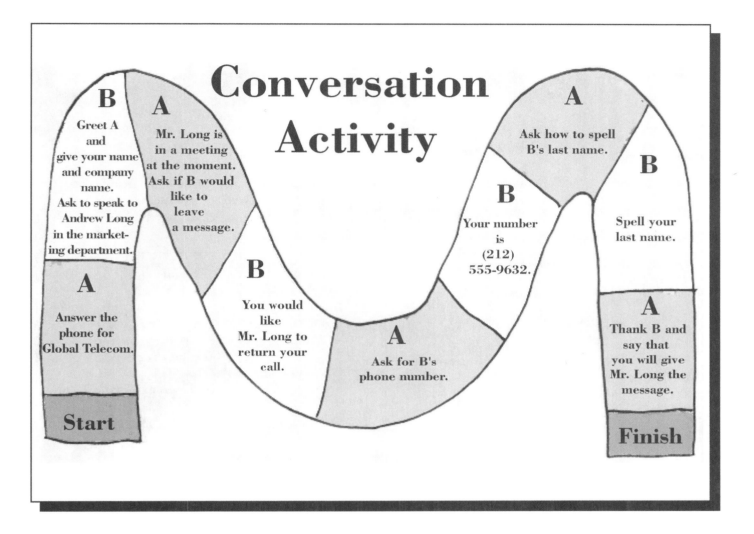

Conversation Activity

B — Greet A and give your name and company name. Ask to speak to Andrew Long in the marketing department.

A — Mr. Long is in a meeting at the moment. Ask if B would like to leave a message.

A — Answer the phone for Global Telecom.

Start

B — You would like Mr. Long to return your call.

A — Ask for B's phone number.

B — Your number is (212) 555-9632.

A — Ask how to spell B's last name.

B — Spell your last name.

A — Thank B and say that you will give Mr. Long the message.

Finish

3. Think of a real situation at your place of work in which you will have to make a phone call in English. Who would you call? What would be the purpose of the call? What would you talk about? Write a short conversation of a realistic telephone situation. Then, practice your conversation with a colleague.

   ➤ Use language from the module to make your conversations sound natural and realistic.

Communication Activities

1. In pairs, role-play the following telephone conversation. One person takes the part of Sung-Wook Jung and refers to File 10. The other person takes the part of Terry Smith, procurement manager for Cellular Technology, Inc., and refers to File 13.

2. Your colleague has set up an appointment to meet with you, but you have to cancel. Ask for your partner's phone number. Then call your partner and leave a message on his or her answering machine or voice mail. Include the following information.

    •   Your name and phone number
    •   The date and time you are calling
    •   Your reason for calling—"I'm calling to let you know . . ."
    •   Say that you have to cancel your appointment.
    •   Give a good reason for canceling the appointment.
    •   Say that you will call back to reschedule the appointment.
    •   Apologize for canceling and say good-bye.

3. Role-play the following telephone situations with a colleague. One person takes A and the other B. Think about your part and make notes of useful language before beginning the call. Then change roles for the second conversation.

A: Ted Thatcher

You have just been laid off at work and are extremely upset.
You feel like you have given your company five of your best years. You really need to talk to someone about this, so you call your good friend Jack Thompson.

B: Jack Thompson

You are in the middle of preparing notes for a report you have to present in 30 minutes.
You feel frustrated because you don't have all the data you need to make your point. This presentation is very important for your career advancement.

Your phone rings. Ted Thatcher, one of your best friends, is on the line.

A: Jean Booker

You will be traveling to Dallas, Texas, next week on business and need to rent a car for five days. Call National Car Rental and find out the rate for a midsized car for five days, insurance, and any other fees.
If the rates are reasonable, make a reservation. Be ready to give your credit card information.

B: Pat Rogers at National Car Rental

Answer the phone and provide any requested information.
The daily rate for a midsized car is $35.
Accident insurance costs an additional $5 per day. The weekly rate is $200 for the rental and $30 for insurance. If the caller is interested, you can make a reservation with a credit card. Be sure to get the name, credit card number, and expiration date. Give the caller this confirmation number: 4PQ27832.

Module 4

Traveling
Internationally

Unit 13

Making Plans

Li-ting Wang is the marketing manager for TaiCom International, Ltd., a Taiwanese company that manufactures personal computers, computer peripherals, and components. He is meeting with two of his marketing associates, Leslie Fong from the Singapore office and Richard Lee from the Hong Kong office, to discuss two upcoming trade shows.

peripherals: equipment used with computers
components: any of the main parts

Read about the two trade shows. With a colleague, discuss the differences between the two shows and their advantages.

Consumer Electronics Show

January 8–11
Las Vegas, Nevada, USA

No. of Exhibitors: 2,000
Square Meters: 87,500
No. of Attendees: 100,000
Foreign Attendance: 12%
Foreign Exhibitors: 44%

Event Description: International CES is a showcase dedicated solely to consumer electronics products. CES attracts more influential buyers and decision makers in the consumer electronics industry than any other trade show.

Exhibitor Information: Manufacturers and distributors of consumer electronic products: audio, video, car audio, computer hardware and software accessories, satellite earth stations, telephones, calculators, watches, cameras, home office products, home theater, mobile electronics and home and auto security.

Attendee Information: Attendees include people involved in the manufacturing, retailing, wholesaling, servicing and importing/exporting of consumer electronics products (i.e., retailers, distributors, manufacturers, institutional buyers, manufacturers' reps, advertising, marketing, PR consultants and financial market analysts).

Comdex UK
Oct. 6–8 at Earls Court 2, London, England

No. of Exhibitors: 327
Square Meters: 13,299
No. of Attendees: 27,468
Foreign Attendance: 11%
Foreign Exhibitors: 14%

Event Description: COMDEX UK will be a technology trade show of unprecedented scope and quality. This event will bring together COMDEX, Networld/Interop and EXPO COMM, creating the first-ever forum focused on converging information technology, networking and telecommunications markets.

COMDEX: the IT industry's #1 showcase and launching pad for new and emerging technologies. It is the only business-to-business computer exposition in the U.K.
NETWORLD+INTEROP: the industry's leading showcase and conference dedicated to internetworking technologies, applications and solutions.
EXPO COMM: the premier worldwide event for telecommunications infrastructure technologies, communications services, and related applications.

This joint exhibition and conference allows industry professionals to see all of the latest technologies in their fields and network with IT directors, developers, technical specialists, IT consultants, and industry analysts.

International Travel

In groups, talk about the problems that can occur when traveling internationally. Then, give advice about the following concerns.

Example: To avoid getting serious jet lag, it is a good idea to get on the schedule of the country you will be visiting before you even leave home. It's also advisable to drink lots of water on the plane.

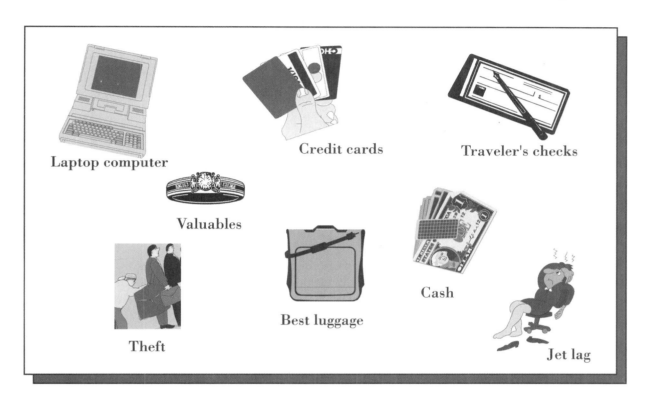

Laptop computer   Credit cards   Traveler's checks

Valuables

Theft   Best luggage   Cash   Jet lag

 Listening Practice

Mr. Wang is talking with Ms. Fong and Mr. Lee at TaiCom's headquarters in Taipei, Taiwan.

A. Listen and check (✓) true or false for each statement as Mr. Wang and his colleagues talk about the two shows. If the sentence is false, change it to make it true.

	True	False
1. TaiCom is planning on exhibiting at both the show in the United States and the show in England.	❏	❏
2. They have already made a decision to exhibit at the World PC Expo in Japan.	❏	❏
3. They decided on the show in London because it opens the door to the European market.	❏	❏
4. The TaiCom executives are interested in U.S. retailers as potential customers.	❏	❏
5. One important difference is that the two shows represent two separate markets.	❏	❏

B. Listen again and discuss your answers to the following questions.

1. Which trade show is more attractive to the TaiCom managers? Give two reasons.
2. What do the TaiCom marketing managers want to accomplish by attending the Consumer Electronics Show?

C. Match the expressions on the left with the best meaning on the right. Refer to the conversation or the trade show descriptions for help.

1. __ to get our foot in the door   a. to gain entry or acceptance

2. __ priorities   b. showy, attracting a lot of attention

3. __ distributor   c. the place where a conference is held

4. __ retailer   d. limitations

5. __ venue   e. the arrangement of items in order of importance

6. __ glitzy   f. one who delivers goods from the manufacturer to the retailer

7. __ constraints   g. one who sells to the final consumer

Key Language

Listen, repeat, and practice aloud with a partner.

Discussing Plans	**Response**
What are your plans for exhibits next year?	We're planning to exhibit at two shows next year.
What are you planning to do this evening?	I'm going out to dinner with a client.
Do you have plans for Saturday afternoon?	No, not really—we're just taking it easy.

Talking about Similarities and Differences
Comparing both shows, the biggest difference is size.
The Consumer Electronics Show is more expensive than COMDEX.
There are four times as many attendees at CES as at COMDEX.
Another difference is that these shows represent two separate markets for us.
The main similarity is that many of the big name companies will be exhibiting at both shows.

Talking about Advantages and Disadvantages
One big advantage of exhibiting at CES is that we can meet retailers from all over the United States.
On the other hand, many of the big retailers will also be at the COMDEX show.
The only drawback of CES is the cost. It's going to be quite expensive.

Coming to a Decision	**Response**
All right then, why don't we get a booth at the Las Vegas show?	Sounds like a solid plan to me.
Do you agree with that plan?	Yes, I think that's the right decision.

Language Mastery

1. **Discussing Plans:** Ask the following questions to a colleague.

   a. What are your plans for the weekend?
   b. Do you have any plans for this evening?
   c. What activities is your department currently planning?
   d. What plans do you have for this week? month? year?
   e. What are your company's short and long range plans?

2. **Making Comparisons:** Make simple comparisons as in the example.

   > *Note:* Use *even* when something is a surprising result or piece of information.

   Example: The Pentium II computers are powerful. (Pentium III)
                 That's true, but the Pentium III computers are even more powerful.

   a. A Porsche is fast. (a Lambourgini)
   b. Los Angeles has a lot of people. (Mexico City)
   c. Frank is a successful businessman. (Roger)
   d. It's cheap to call long distance these days. (use e-mail)

   e. Her assistant has a good salary. (her boss)

   f. Jennifer is an ambitious sales manager. (Susan)

   g. It is expensive to take the train from Paris to Frankfurt. (to fly)

   h. Our profits are bad this month. (last month)

   i. Housing costs are high in Denver. (the San Francisco Bay area)

   j. The presentation this morning was interesting. (yesterday's presentation)

3. Listen to the sentences and check the type of comparison being made.

Example: Our marketing budget for this year will be far more than last year's. (much more)

	Much More	More	The Same	Less (or fewer)	Much Less (or many fewer)
a.	❏	❏	❏	❏	❏
b.	❏	❏	❏	❏	❏
c.	❏	❏	❏	❏	❏
d.	❏	❏	❏	❏	❏
e.	❏	❏	❏	❏	❏
f.	❏	❏	❏	❏	❏
g.	❏	❏	❏	❏	❏
h.	❏	❏	❏	❏	❏

4. **Talking about Advantages and Disadvantages:** With a colleague, take turns talking about the advantages and disadvantages of the following topics. One of you will be A and the other B. Use this conversation as a model.

   A: The main advantage of credit cards is that you don't have to carry a lot of money around with you.

   B: That's true, but the disadvantage is that it's hard to keep track of what you're spending, so many people overspend and go into debt.

   A: That's a drawback, but the best thing about credit cards is that they are accepted everywhere these days.

   B: You're absolutely right, but the problem is that credit cards make people think they have more money than they really do.

a.	credit cards	d.	traveling on business
b.	cellular phones	e.	investing in stocks
c.	attending trade shows	f.	working for yourself

TOEIC Tip

Comparisons

Comparisons are used frequently in business communication, and they are also covered in the grammar and listening sections of the TOEIC exam.

Add *-er* to adjectives with one syllable: big → bigger
Add *more* before adjectives with more than one syllable: expensive → more expensive
Add *more* or *less* / fewer before a noun: more memory, less money, fewer resources

> *Note:*   Use *less* before noncount nouns, *fewer* before count nouns.
> There is less money in the bank today.
> Fewer people enrolled in the course than last session.

Superlatives
Add *the* + *-est* to adjectives with one syllable: big → the biggest
Add *the* + *most* / *least* before adjectives with 2+ syllables: expensive → the most expensive

Talking about Large and Small Differences
He works much longer each day than I do. (large difference)
There were a few more people at the meeting this week than last week. (small difference)
Far more people work at the Taipei factory than at the Kaoshiung factory. (large difference)
TECHPro isn't as successful as it used to be.

Quantitative Comparisons
There are four times as many exhibitors at CES as at COMDEX.
Laptop computers are twice as expensive as desktop PCs.
Los Angeles is about three times the size of Salt Lake City.
Kaoshiung is about half the size of Taipei.

5. With a colleague, discuss similarities and differences between the words in the sets below.

Example: A <u>friend</u> is someone whom you like, know very well, and spend time with. In contrast, an <u>acquaintance</u> is someone whom you have merely met. You know this person's name and may interact socially from time to time, but you do not spend much time together.

a.	accounting	finance
b.	friend	acquaintance
c.	company	corporation
d.	stocks	bonds
e.	gross revenue	net revenue
f.	company mission	company vision

Unit 14

Making Airline Reservations

Leslie Fong, TaiCom's marketing representative in Singapore, calls United Airlines to check on flight availability for the Las Vegas trip.

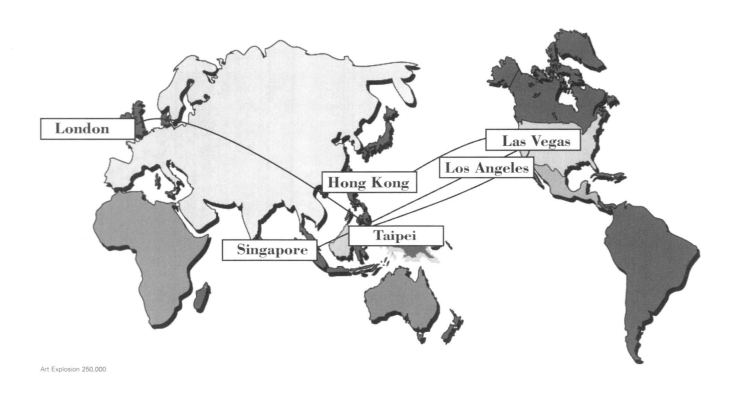

Art Explosion 250,000

Listening Practice

A. Leslie takes notes as she talks to a United Airlines ticketing agent. Listen and fill in the missing information.

Singapore – Las Vegas Trip Reservation #____

Flight # _____

Leaves Singapore at _____ on January 6th.

Arrives in Las Vegas at _____ on_____.

Return Flight #344

Leaves Las Vegas at _____ on January_____.

Arrives in Singapore at 11:45 on_____.

Price of the round-trip ticket: U.S.$ _____.

Length of flight: _____.

B. Listen again and fill in the blanks.

Agent: United International Desk, this is Sally. How _____ ?

Ms. Fong: Yes, I'd like _____ from Singapore to Las Vegas, Nevada.

Agent: When are you _____ ?

Ms. Fong: I do have some flexibility, but I need to be in Las Vegas _____ _____ and return on the 12th.

Agent: Let's see. We have a _____ to Las Vegas with one-hour stops in Tokyo and Los Angeles. You could leave Singapore _____ on January 6th, arriving in Las Vegas at 12:36 P.M. the same day.

Ms. Fong: And what about the return?

Agent: You'd leave Las Vegas on _____ A.M. on January 12th, arriving in Singapore _____ the following day.

Ms. Fong: How _____ ?

Agent: Nineteen hours and thirty-six minutes.

Ms. Fong: Boy, that's a long flight! And how much is it?

Agent: The round-trip ticket is _____ .

Ms. Fong: OK, I think I'd like to go ahead and make a reservation.

Agent: All right, Ms. Fong, your reservation number is

_____ . I can hold

this reservation for 24 hours.

C. Practice the conversation with a colleague until you can say it easily.

➤ Read each line silently. Then look at your partner when speaking.

D. Discuss the meaning of these travel terms with a colleague. Ask your instructor or a native speaker if you need help.

1. itinerary
2. round trip
3. frequent flyer miles
4. coach
5. economy class

6. first class
7. business class
8. upgrade
9. baggage carousel
10. charter flight

 Key Language

Listen, repeat, and practice aloud with a partner.

Asking for Flight Information   **Response**
I would like to check on flight availability
     from Singapore to Las Vegas, Nevada.
I would like some information about flights
     from Hong Kong to San Francisco.
How long is the flight?
Do I need to change planes in Tokyo?
Where do I go through customs?
Is there a charge if I need to change my plans?   Yes, there is a $75.00 charge.
OK, I'd like to book a flight.
I'd like to go ahead and make a reservation.

Asking about Travel Plans   **Response**
When are you planning on traveling?   I need to be in Las Vegas by January 7th
                                                                              and return on the 12th.

Could you travel on the 6th?   If I can get to Las Vegas by the 7th.

Asking about Price   **Response**
How much is the ticket?   The round-trip airfare is U.S.$1,044.
How much does a one-way ticket cost?   A one-way ticket costs $939.00.

Note: A direct flight may make short stops, but you do not need to change planes. On a nonstop flight, there are no stops.

Language Mastery

1. With a colleague, take turns being the customer and the ticketing agent. If you are the customer, ask questions to find out the following information. When necessary, make up logical responses.

   a. information about flights from Taipei to Los Angeles
   b. how long the flight will last (9 1/2 hours)
   c. the price of a round-trip ticket (U.S.$1,456)
   d. where you will go through customs (Los Angeles)
   e. the flight number (UA 994)
   f. the arrival time in Los Angeles (6:30 P.M.)
   g. which airport the plane flies into in Washington, D.C. (Dulles or National)
   h. changing planes
   i. the charge for changing flight plans ($75.00)
   j. the use of frequent flyer miles on this flight

 2. A. Listen to the conversation with a travel agent and fill in the missing information.

```
○  ○  ○  ○  ○  ○  ○
            n o t e s


Destination: _____


Departure Date: _____


Number in Party: _____


Hotel Preference: _____


Special Requests: _____

_____
```

B. Summarize the conversation with a partner.

3. Mr. Wang is staying in San Francisco for two nights on business before going to the trade show in Las Vegas. At the airport, he asks how to get to his hotel in the city. Listen to the conversation and write the three ways to get from the San Francisco Airport to the Hyatt Hotel.

Transportation from the San Francisco Airport to the Hyatt Hotel on Market Street

Cost

1. _____   _____

2. _____   _____

3. _____   _____

4. A. After Mr. Wang gets to his hotel in San Francisco, he goes to the bar to have a drink. Listen as he describes his last trip to Miami, Florida.

B. Now discuss with a colleague what you would do in each of those circumstances.

5. These are Mr. Wang's travel plans: leave Taipei, Taiwan, on January 5th for San Francisco; spend two days in San Francisco on business; fly to Las Vegas on January 7th; and then return to Taipei on January 12th. Call a U.S. airline company and find out the information needed for his itinerary, including times, stops, and cost. Once you have this information, try this phone call with a colleague. One person plays the part of Mr. Wang of TaiCom. The other plays the part of a ticketing agent.

Unit 15

Booking a Hotel, Checking In, and Checking Out

Leslie Fong of TaiCom is talking to a travel agent about hotels in the Las Vegas area.

 Listening Practice

A. Listen and fill in the missing information about each hotel.

	Caesar's Palace	Mirage	Triple Crown
Proximity to the Convention Center	_____	Three blocks	_____
Price per night for a single room	$275.00	_____	_____
Amenities/Facilities	business services, swimming pool, _____ gambling, nightly shows	business services, swimming pool, health spa and salon, gym, _____ _____ gourmet restaurants, free parking, gambling, nightly shows, shopping, a tropical rain forest, and a giant aquarium	business services, _____ gambling
Number of Rooms	_____	_____	800
Complimentary Breakfast	continental breakfast	_____ _____	_____

78

amenities: things that add to people's comfort, convenience, pleasure
complimentary: free (no charge)

B. Write and then ask a colleague five questions comparing these hotels. Write your questions on a separate piece of paper. If you need help, refer to the Language Notes, page 177.

Example: Which hotel is the most expensive?

 ## Key Language

Listen, repeat, and practice aloud with a partner.

Making a Reservation
Do you have a room available January 6th through the 11th? (= leaving the morning of the 12th)
What is the rate per night?

I'd like to make a reservation, please.

Response
Yes, we do. Would you like a single or a double?
The rate for a single is $183.00 per night.
Certainly. Your name?

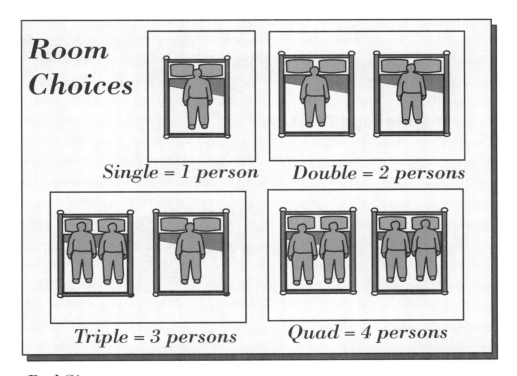

Room Choices

Single = 1 person   Double = 2 persons

Triple = 3 persons   Quad = 4 persons

Bed Sizes

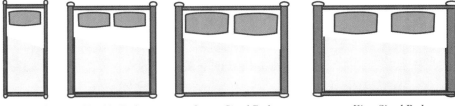

Twin Bed   *Double Bed*   *Queen-Sized Bed*   *King-Sized Bed*

Checking In
I'd like to check in. The name is Bradshaw.
I have a reservation. My name is Leslie Fong.

Response
Let's see. Yes, I have your reservation.
One moment. Oh yes. I have your
    reservation, Ms. Fong.

Common Questions When Checking In
Smoking or non?
Would you like a minibar key? (minibar = a small
    refrigerator with drinks and snacks)
Would you like a king or two queens?
Could I make an imprint of your card?
Would you like help with your luggage?
How many keys to your room?

Response
Nonsmoking, thank you.
Yes, please.

I'd prefer a king, thanks.
Certainly.
Yes, please. / No, thanks.
Just one, please.

Checking Out
I'd like to check out, please. My room is 2423.
Could I please have an itemized copy of the bill?
Do you have express checkout?

Response
One moment while I get your bill.
Certainly. It'll be just a moment.
Yes. You can see your charges and
    check out on the TV in your
    room.

Notes:
1. Give a tip of one dollar per bag if a bellhop takes your bags to your room.
2. When checking out, be sure to get an itemized copy of your bill.

Language Mastery

1. With a colleague, take turns asking and answering these questions.

    a. What kind of a hotel do you prefer on business trips? (A luxury hotel?
        A full-service hotel? A motel? A bed and breakfast?)
    b. How important is the location?
    c. What amenities or facilities are particularly important for you?
    d. What are some of the main hotel chains in your country? Do you have a
        preference?

2. **Checking into a Hotel:** Listen as Leslie Fong checks into the Mirage.
    Check (✓) true or false for each statement. If the choice is false,
    rewrite the sentence to make it correct.

	True	False
a. When Leslie checks into the hotel, they find her reservation easily.	❏	❏
b. She will be staying six nights.	❏	❏

c.	The rate per night is $229.00.	❏	❏

d.	She requests two double beds.	❏	❏

e.	Her room is on the twenty-fourth floor.	❏	❏

f.	She wants help with her luggage.	❏	❏

3. **Using Hotel Services:** Who would you call to make these requests at a hotel: the front desk, the bell captain, the concierge, housekeeping, room service? Go through the list with a partner and then practice what you would say.

Who would you call?

a. order dinner in your room   _____

b. request a late checkout   _____

c. have someone call a taxi for you   _____

d. get your suit cleaned   _____

e. request an iron and ironing board   _____

f. order cocktails for guests in your suite   _____

g. ask how to make a long-distance call   _____

h. request a wake-up call   _____

i. turn the air conditioning down   _____

j. inquire about a good restaurant for dinner   _____

> **concierge:** a person in a hotel who sits in the lobby and helps guests with problems or answers questions

4. You are calling to make a reservation for yourself and two of your colleagues at the Mirage Hotel in Las Vegas. Work in pairs. One person looks at File 12 on page 158; the other looks at File 16 on page 160.

5. **Checking out of a Hotel:** Listen as Leslie Fong checks out of her hotel. What are two charges that she questions?

a. _____

b. _____

Unit 16

Describing Products at a Trade Show

Mr. Wang is talking with Sarah Adams, a customer, at TaiCom's booth at the Consumer Electronics Trade Show in Las Vegas.

Photo Credit: Las Vegas Convention and Visitors Authority

 Listening Practice

A. Listen to the conversation as you read the text.

Mr. Wang:	Can _____ ?
Sarah Adams:	Well, yes. I've been to this show several times, and I haven't seen TaiCom before. Is this_____ ?
Mr. Wang:	Yes, as a matter of fact. We've only been in business for a few years and have been concentrating primarily on Asia up to this point.
Sarah Adams:	Well, I hope it _____ . By the way, I'm Sarah Adams, purchasing manager for Computer City. So tell me about your computers.
Mr. Wang:	Hi, Sarah. How do you do? I'm Li-ting Wang. Well, you can find anything you want at this show, but where we really excel is in _____ at a great price.
Sarah Adams:	We're always _____ . How do your prices compare with Compaq's, for example?
Mr. Wang:	_____, and with the exchange rates what they are right now, we're a terrific value.
Sarah Adams:	Well, that sounds interesting. Listen, I don't have much time right now—but I'd be _____ in more detail when I get home.
Mr. Wang:	Great. Here, _____ , a price list, and some literature about our products to take with you.

Sarah Adams: Oh, thanks. And here's my card.

Mr. Wang: _____, and I'll give you a call

when I get back.

> **to concentrate on:** to focus attention on
> **distinctive:** different, unique
> **to excel:** to be superior in a given area

B. Practice the conversation with a colleague until you can say it easily.

➤ Read each line silently. Then look at your partner when speaking.

C. Mr. Wang had only a few minutes to talk to Sarah Adams. Discuss with your colleague what strategies he used to be effective in promoting his products in a short period of time. What else could he have done?

 ## Key Language

Listen, repeat, and practice aloud.

Small Talk at a Trade Show
Can I answer any questions?
How's the show going for you?

Describing Product Strengths
Our computers have very high performance at a good price.
We offer enhanced functionality and performance at a good value.
The main qualities we emphasize are reliability, high performance, and value.

Describing a Product or Service (Specifications)

Performance
Our 4800 multimedia computer runs on an Intel Pentium III processor with
    MMX technology. It has a 40-gigabyte hard drive and 933 megahertz.
The Hewlett Packard Deskjet 600C printer prints 12 pages per minute.

Features
This computer has the following features: DVD-ROM drive, 56K modem,
    a fast Ethernet card, a CD writer, and 3D sound.
The Hewlett Packard printer has scalable TrueType fonts, I/O interface, and
    2400 × 1200 dpi.

Physical Characteristics
Our laptop computer has a 13.3-inch screen and weighs 5 pounds.
The Hewlett Packard Deskjet 600C printer weighs 11.6 pounds (5.3 kg).
The dimensions of the printer are 17.2 inches wide by 7.9 inches high by 16 inches
    deep.
Qualities: reliable, efficient, high quality, economical

Note: Rather than *cheap,* use *economical* or *a good value.*

Language Mastery

1. Ask your colleague the following questions; then your partner will ask you the questions. Go through the list twice.

   a. Describe a recent product you purchased.
   b. What features, qualities, performance did it have that influenced your decision?
   c. How important was the brand name?
   d. Compare your product to competitive products.
   e. What one factor was most important in influencing your decision?

2. **Describing Products:** Work in groups and describe these products. This is a brainstorming session, so offer as many ideas as possible. Talk about what the product is used for, its physical characteristics, special features, qualities, and so on.

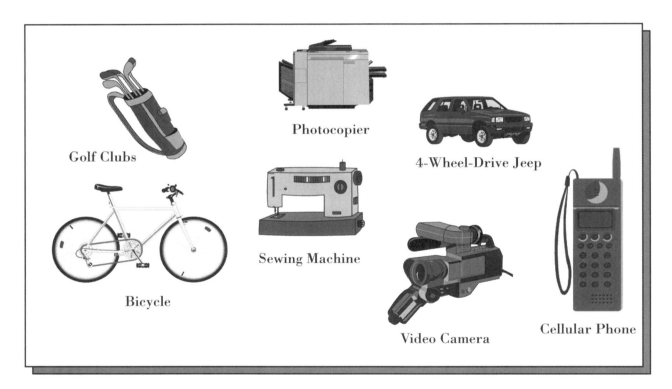

Golf Clubs

Photocopier

4-Wheel-Drive Jeep

Bicycle

Sewing Machine

Video Camera

Cellular Phone

3. To play this game, form two teams. Each team will think of several consumer products. Decide on one product first. The other team then will begin by asking up to ten *yes* or *no* questions about the product. If a team guesses the product, it gets 1 point. Then, the other team has a chance. Keep score to find out who wins.

4. After the Las Vegas electronics trade show, a major U.S. retailer, Computer City, is calling to get information about TaiCom's new multimedia desktop computer. In pairs, try the conversation using your real names. One person will be the marketing manager for TaiCom International and refer to File 20 on page 162. The other person will be Computer City's purchasing manager and refer to File 36 on page 171. When you finish, change roles and try it again.

Professional Protocol

Business cards are used in professional interactions throughout the world. However, the way they are used differs from country to country. In groups, discuss how business cards are used in your countries.

How are cards printed? If you are doing international business, do you have your cards printed in more than one language? Do you print on both sides?
How and when are business cards presented?

Guidelines for Using Business Cards in the United States

Your business card is a very important part of your professional communication. When you give it to someone, it says, "I care about our relationship, and I want to keep in touch in the future." The following points describe how business cards are used in the United States.

- Always have business cards with you; you never know whom you might meet.
- Only give out cards that are new and in perfect condition.
- At a business reception or in a business/social situation, cards are usually exchanged at the end of a conversation whenever business has been discussed. This is usually a private exchange between two business people.
- A junior executive should wait until a more senior executive asks for his or her card. If you want to give your card to someone, ask for his or her card first. Most people will then ask you for your card in return.
- When you are at a business meeting away from your office, cards may be exchanged at the beginning or at the end, so wait for someone else to begin the exchanging of cards.
- If you are giving a presentation, feel free to give out your cards in the beginning to those in attendance so they will know your name and title.
- If you are at a social dinner, cards should not be exchanged during the meal. In fact, people generally avoid talking about business altogether during dinner.
- Don't pass your card out freely. Be discriminating about whom you give your card to so that people will value your card and the relationship it represents.
- Use business cards to help you remember people. As soon as possible after meeting someone, write notes on the back of the card to help you remember the person you have just met.

Communication Activities

1. **New Product Development:** Work in a group—this is your opportunity to be creative!

   a. You are members of a product development team for a large company. You have been given the task of creating a new product or modifying or improving an existing product that would appeal to the largest number of people. Possible ideas: snack food, electronics product, hairdryer, iron, toaster, vacuum cleaner, lawn mower, calculator, lamp, running shoe, personal care product, and so on.

   b. Choose someone on your team to write down all the ideas that are generated.

c. To begin, select a product category and brainstorm to come up with as many new ideas, new products, or product innovations in your category as possible. Encourage many wild ideas. Actively listen to one another. Keep the pace fast. Don't criticize ideas at this point.

d. Select your top new product idea. Discuss and decide the following.

- What name will you give your product?
- What are the functions, features, dimensions of the product?
- What target market is it intended for?
- What price do you propose for it at first? Why?
- How would you package it?
- Where will it be sold?
- How would you promote it?
- Is your product an economical solution?

e. Make a drawing or an illustration of your product.
f. Present your product concept to the class.

2. An important client will be visiting you for some meetings next week. He or she will be arriving on Thursday afternoon and leaving on Saturday morning. Call two large international hotels in your area and ask about the following.

- The rate per night for a standard single room
- The rate for a suite
- Whether breakfast is included
- The hotel's amenities (meeting rooms, swimming pool, restaurants, business center, athletic gym, etc.)

Report your findings to your group. Make a chart of the leading hotels in your area with rates per night and advantages and disadvantages of each hotel.
In which hotel would you put your guest and why? Consider quality, cost, location, amenities, and so on.

Hotel	Rates per night: A. Standard room B. Suite	Advantages/ Disadvantages	Comments
1.			
2.			

Module 5

Entertaining a Business Associate

Unit 17

A Business Lunch

Edmundo Orsi, who is from Argentina, is in Washington, D.C., this week for an international trade conference. He wants to invite a new business acquaintance, Rick Masterson, to lunch. Edmundo met Rick at a reception a few weeks ago at the Ministry of Trade in Buenos Aires. The two really hit it off and promised to stay in touch. Rick heads the Overseas Export Department at SA Industries, whose auto parts are traded worldwide. Edmundo wants to maintain this relationship with Rick, so he gives Rick a call.

to hit it off: to get along well
to maintain: to continue

 Listening Practice

Listen to the phone call when Edmundo calls Rick. Fill in information about their lunch meeting.

☐ **Wednesday, January 31**

APPOINTMENTS

What: *Lunch Meeting with Edmundo Orsi*

Where: _____

Time: _____

Business Entertainment

Global Cultures
What are the customs in these social business situations in your country?
Discuss in small groups.

1. How do you invite someone for lunch or dinner—in person, on the phone, by e-mail?
2. How do you decide who pays for a business lunch?
3. What is the most common business meal in your country? Is it common for people to do business during a game of golf, tennis, or racquetball?
4. Are you familiar with the expression *power lunch?* What do you think it means?
5. As host or hostess, what can one do to make business guests comfortable in a social situation?

Listening Practice

In the United States, invitations are often informal. People frequently extend invitations over the phone. Listen to these phone invitations left on answering machines. Then fill in the blanks on the invitation below.

1.

You're Invited

WHO: _____

WHAT: _____

WHERE: _____

WHEN: _____

2.

RSVP

WHO: _____

WHAT: _____

WHERE: _____

WHEN: _____

3.

Please Join Us

WHO: _____

WHAT: _____

WHERE: _____

WHEN: _____

 Key Language

Listen, repeat, and practice aloud with a partner.

Inviting Someone to Lunch/Dinner
What are you doing for lunch tomorrow?
Well, let's have lunch. We could try that
   new Thai restaurant close to your office.

Sure. How about Thursday or Friday?
What about having dinner downtown
   tonight?
Let's do lunch sometime.
   (= have lunch together)

Accepting/Declining Invitations
Let's see. Tomorrow I'm free.
{ Sounds good. What time works for you?
  Oh, I'm sorry. I just remembered a prior
  engagement. Could we make it another
  day?
Friday's good. Let's count on it.
{ You bet. I'd love to.
  Sorry. I've got plans.
Great. I'll give you a call next week.

You want to get a drink after work?　　$\left\{\begin{array}{l}\text{I'm afraid I can't. I've got something tonight.} \\ \text{Oh, I'm busy this evening. Another time?} \\ \text{That'd be great. Where shall we go?}\end{array}\right.$

❖ What does *'d* mean in the expression　*That'd be great?*

Making Reservations at a Restaurant　　　　　**Response**
I'd like to make a reservation for lunch today.　　Sure. Your name, please?
Steve Waters.　　　　　　　　　　　　　　　　　And how many in your party, Mr. Waters?
Two. I'd like to make the reservation for 12:30.　All right. We'll see you at 12:30.

Notes:
1. *Sometime,* as in the expression *Let's have lunch sometime,* doesn't give a specific time. This expression means that the person is interested in spending some time together at lunch. It is not a definite invitation. If you want to follow up, say something specific: "Yes, I'll give you a call next week" *or* "I'm free most of this week. Let me know when is good for you." If you are not sure about the invitation, you could say, "Yes, give me a call [sometime]."
2. Indirect invitations are also common: *I wonder if you'd like to join us for a beer after work?*

Language Mastery

1. In pairs, practice giving and responding to invitations. One person asks the questions in File 15 on page 160. The second person asks the questions in File 17 on page 161.
2. In pairs, take turns inviting each other to do the items in the list below. Accept or decline based on your interests.

   Example:　　have lunch after you get back from your trip
   　　　　　　　　A: What about having lunch after you get back from your trip?
   　　　　　　　　B: Sure. That'd be great.

   - have lunch next week
   - play "Go" this afternoon
   - go out for drinks tomorrow evening
   - play tennis when the weather improves

   - get some coffee during the break
   - have dinner one day this week
   - go running at lunchtime on Friday
   - try a game of racquetball sometime

   Your Suggestions

   - _____
   - _____

3. **Inviting:** Extend invitations in these situations. Take turns with a colleague.

1. You're asking a few people to come by your apartment after work this afternoon.	2. You're having a picnic at a beautiful lake this weekend for your team at work. Invite your boss.	3. You're going to give a party for a colleague who has just become a father. Invite your department head.	4. You want to try the new microbrewery that just opened close to work. Invite your business colleague for a drink.	5. You're looking for a tennis partner. Invite your new co-worker to play sometime soon. Suggest a day and time.
6. You're organizing a small reception for an international guest. Invite your colleague from the 15th floor.	7. You're giving a dinner at your home in a week. Invite your office mate.	8. You're looking for someone to practice golf with. You just want to practice hitting. Ask an office mate.	9. You're on the phone with a client from New Orleans, where you will be in two days. Invite the client to dinner Friday.	10. You're going to start walking every day at lunchtime. Invite a colleague to join you.

4. **Inviting:** Think of one activity that you really like: sports, shopping, outdoor recreation, studying, something computer related. Think of one or two people to join you in this activity. If possible, try to ask someone who doesn't speak your language. When the timing is good, invite someone to do the activity with you—even if it is only to walk to a bookstore. Make a conscious effort to extend one or more invitations. In a week, get together with a small group in your class to compare experiences.

Professional Protocol

Guidelines for Restaurant Dining
Compare these tips about restaurant dining in the United States to customs in your country.

Dining Out
- When you arrive at the restaurant, the receptionist will ask for your reservation. You can say:

  I'm Yoshi Kitanohara. I have a reservation for 12:30.
  I've got a reservation for 7:00. The name is Park.

- The waitperson at a good restaurant will want to tell you about the specials (special dishes for the day). You will hear a fast description of several dishes that is challenging to understand: "The chef's special tonight is chateaubriand—beef tenderloin prepared rare, medium rare, or medium and served with sauce béarnaise and parsley potatoes."

  Tip: If you can listen for the type of food, whether it's fish or meat, that is a good start.

  Then you could ask your dining partner about it: "How's the fish dish prepared?"

- When you are ready to order your food, the waitperson will ask:

  May I take your order now? (*or*) Have you decided? (*or*) Are you ready to order?
  You could say: Could you give us a few more minutes? (*or*) Yes, we're ready.

Wine

- People in the United States often order wine with dinner. The person who orders the wine is expected to sample and approve of the bottle. A small amount of wine is poured for you to taste. After tasting, you can tell the server: "Yes, that's nice. Thank you." You can send a wine back only if it has turned to vinegar, which is rare. If you don't like the wine, this isn't a good reason to return it.

  Tip: If you are not familiar with wines, ask your dinner companion(s) or the restaurant staff for a recommendation. Decide on your food first. Generally, order a red wine with beef and tomato-based sauces; order white wine with fish, light meats, and vegetable plates.

Payment and Tipping

- Payment is usually by credit card. A restaurant often requires two forms of identification to take your personal check drawn on a local bank. Cash is less common.

- Since restaurant workers usually make low wages, they depend on receiving tips. A tip of 15–20 percent of the total bill is added by the customer to the credit card bill total or left on the table in cash. If service isn't satisfactory, a smaller tip is left.

  Tip: For large groups, the tip is sometimes included. Look for this note on the menu: "For parties of eight or more, a gratuity of 20 percent will be added to the total." This means the restaurant will add the tip to your bill; you don't need to leave extra cash.

- Restaurant staff will often use abbreviated language when talking about prices. For example, they sometimes mention the prices of the specials. If they don't, you should ask:

  How much is the shellfish special?
  It's 16. (= It's 16 dollars.) (*or*) It's 14.50. (= It's 14 dollars and 50 cents.)

Unit 18

Ordering Food

Edmundo knew it was going to be hard to read the menu at Julia's, but he was astonished when he sat down with Rick. Even Rick had to ask the waiter to explain several items. Identify difficult vocabulary from this menu with a colleague and discuss with your instructor. (See the menu on page 94.)

 Listening Practice

Understanding Food Orders: Listen and identify the food ordered while you look at the menu from Julia's. Each item is spoken twice. The first time, decide if the choice is an appetizer or an entrée; the second time, write which dish is ordered.

1. ☑ appetizer ☐ entrée   *mushrooms with chèvre*

2. ☐ appetizer ☐ entrée _____

3. ☐ appetizer ☐ entrée _____

4. ☐ appetizer ☐ entrée _____

5. ☐ appetizer ☐ entrée _____

6. ☐ appetizer ☐ entrée _____

7. ☐ appetizer ☐ entrée _____

8. ☐ appetizer ☐ entrée _____

 Key Language

Listen, repeat, and practice aloud with a partner.

Ordering Food	Waitperson Response
Are there any specials today?	Yes, we've got a turkey blue plate special for $8.99.
What's the soup of the day?	Split pea.
I'd like the filet mignon.	Yes, sir. How would you like that?
Medium well.	Certainly. And would you care for soup or salad?
Salad.	Dressing?
What kind do you have?	Thousand Island, Italian, French, and blue cheese.
Italian. Could I have it on the side?	Certainly. And baked potato, rice, or French fries?
A baked potato, please.	Butter and sour cream?
Yes, please.	Anything else?
Could we get some more water?	Sure. I'll be right there.

Julia's

Classic and Contemporary Cuisine
French • Italian • Spanish • American

Appetizers

• Mushrooms with Chèvre & Rosemary

• Terrine of Eggplant with Roasted Red Pepper

• Lobster-Shrimp Ravioli

• Cajun Spiced Calamari

• Gnocchi Verde

• Pan Grilled Radicchio with Crispy Fried Eggplant Ravioli

Dinner Entrées

Entrées are $19.50–$23.75, served with soup or salad and vegetables.

• Filet Mignon with Stilton Ale Sauce

• Salmon Fillet with Garlic-Lime Sauce

• Mariscos Viscaina

• Shrimp Nancy

• Fettuccine with Roast Duck & Portobellos

• Pork Tenderloin with Roasted Garlic

• Wild Mushroom Polenta with Asiago Cheese

Julia's Restaurant is charmingly small & chef-owned, serving Washington, D.C., since 1946.
The dress is casual and the service is friendly. Reservations are welcomed.

"Taste & Tastefulness Unite"

Questions and Requests

Do you have a wine list?
We're ready for the check, please.
Could we get the check when you
    have a moment?
Do you take Visa?
Do you take traveler's checks?
Do you take out of state checks?

Waitperson Response

Yes, we do. Let me get one for you.
Yes, I'll be right with you.
Yes, I'll be right back with it.

Yes, Visa, MasterCard, or American Express.
Yes, with a picture ID. (= identification)
I'm sorry. We don't.

Language Mastery

1. How many of these items can you identify? With a partner, name the items in the picture and explain briefly. Use the list below. Then check your answers in File 19, page 162.

    Example: 1. That's a saucepan. It's used in general cooking. The second item is a frying pan, which is used to cook foods in oil.

spoon
salt and pepper
wine in an ice bucket
oil and vinegar
✓frying pan
napkin
water glass
place setting
✓saucepan
butter and butter knife
wineglass
dinner fork
soy sauce
bottle opener
knife
mustard
dinner plate
coffee mug
coffee cup and saucer
cream and sugar
corkscrew
teapot
ketchup
pitcher of water
salad fork
basket of bread
coffeepot
dessert spoon
six-pack of soda
bread plate

2. In small groups, think of different examples of each food category and write them in this chart. Start with items from Julia's Restaurant; then add your own examples. The group with the longest list overall after 10 minutes wins.

Vegetables	Fish	Shellfish	Meat

3. With a partner, group these food items using these categories: ways to cook meat, ways to cook eggs, types of salad dressing, and how long meat is cooked. Work on a separate piece of paper. Use a dictionary and ask your colleague and instructor about items you don't know. Then compare work with another pair.

poached	grilled	Thousand Island	scrambled
medium	Italian	sautéed	medium rare
ranch	barbecued	sunny-side up	blue cheese
rare	over easy	roasted	smoked
oil and vinegar	creamy Italian	baked	hard boiled
fried	soft boiled	well done	vinaigrette

4. **Ordering a Meal:** Look again at the menu from Julia's and decide what to order for dinner. A colleague will role-play the waitperson so you can practice ordering. Because specific prices aren't given on this menu, be sure to ask how much your entrée is. Your partner will make up a price between $19.50 and $23.75. Then reverse roles and see what your colleague orders. Extend this practice by inviting someone to go to a restaurant where you can order in English.

Unit 19

Ordering Drinks

 Listening Practice

A. Edmundo and Rick ordered drinks after they had decided what to order for lunch. Listen and then practice this conversation with a colleague until you can say it easily.

➤ Read each line silently. Then look at your partner when speaking.

Edmundo:	What would you like to drink?
Rick:	I think I'll just have some iced tea.
Edmundo:	Excuse me. What do you have on tap?
Waitperson:	Bud, Bud Light, Miller, Miller Light, Moosehead, and Guinness Stout.
Edmundo:	OK. Let's see. Iced tea for my friend, and I'll have a Moosehead.
Waitperson:	All right. I'll be right back with your drinks.
Rick:	Uh, you know, a Moosehead sounds great. I'd like to change my order.
Waitperson:	So, two Mooseheads?
Rick:	Yeah. Thanks.
Waitperson:	You bet. Back in a moment with your drinks.

on tap: on draft, fresh
you bet: sure, yes

B. Ask your colleague about the following: (1) favorite cold and hot weather drinks, (2) favorite beers, (3) what kind of wine he or she likes, (4) if he or she likes mixed drinks, (5) if he or she likes a favorite national drink such as soju or sake.

> *Note:* When you ask about alcoholic drinks, say, "Do you drink?"
> (= Do you drink alcoholic beverages?)

Listening Practice

Listen to some people ordering drinks at a restaurant. Fill in the drink order below. Then listen again to check your work.

The Oasis Bar & Grill
Washington, D.C.
(212) 555-9000
Guest Check

Qty	Food or Beverage Item
	Subtotal: _____
	Tax: _____
	Total: [	]

Guest Receipt

Date	Amount	
		116948

Key Language

Listen, repeat, and practice aloud with a partner.

Ordering Drinks	**Response**
What kind of soft drinks do you have?	Sprite, Pepsi, root beer, and cream soda.
Would you like a cocktail? (= mixed drink)	Yes, I'll have a scotch on the rocks. (= with ice)
May I see some ID?	Sure, here's my driver's license.
What have you got on tap / on draft?	Coors and Coors Light.
I'll have a Coors.	OK.
Could we get a pitcher of pale ale?	Coming right up. (= I'll bring it to you right away.)
I'd like a bottle of Foster's.	All right.

Soft Drinks
cola (Coke, Pepsi, Diet Coke, Diet Pepsi)
lemon lime soda (Sprite, 7-Up)
ginger ale, root beer, raspberry soda
milk, orange juice, V8 (= tomato and vegetable juice)
mineral water, tonic water, club soda
coffee, tea, iced tea, lemonade, iced cappuccino

Beers
pale ale
amber ale
red ale
lager
malt liquor
light

Wines	**Reds**	**Liquors**	**Mixed Drinks**
red	Cabernet	vodka	gin and tonic
white	Merlot	tequila	margarita
rosé	Chianti	rum	rum and cola
champagne		gin	screwdriver
port	**Whites**	cognac	daiquiri
sherry	Chardonnay	scotch	scotch and soda
	Chablis	whiskey	

Coffee Drinks

latte (= glass of espresso and steamed milk)

skinny latte (= latte with skim milk)

double tall latte (= 2 shots of espresso)

cappuccino (= cup of espresso and steamed milk)

mocha (= espresso, steamed milk, and chocolate)

Americano (= espresso with boiling water)

> *Note:* Brands of beer: Budweiser, Miller, Coors, Moosehead, Dos Equis, Foster's.
> Brands of wine: Robert Mondavi, Fetzer, Korbel, Chateau de la Tour, Louis Jadot, Chateau Lafite-Rothschild.

Language Mastery

1. Instructor Prep Note: For this guessing activity, give the clues in File 24, page 165 aloud so that the class can guess the answers. Listen and guess what's described from the clues your instructor says.

Example: This is a popular alcoholic drink.
Is it a margarita?

No, it's an alcoholic drink made with tonic water.
Is it a gin and tonic?

No, the drink is made with vodka.
It's got to be a vodka tonic!

2. **Ordering Drinks:** With a colleague, take turns reading the situations aloud. What would you order to drink in each situation? Use the language of ordering as you role-play the waitperson or the customer: *I'd like, I'll have, etc.*

   Example: You're at a nice restaurant and want to order wine to go with your shrimp dish.
   What would you like to drink?
   I'd like a glass of chardonnay, please.

   a. You sit down at the hotel's outdoor restaurant under an umbrella table with your friend. You've just been running and are really thirsty.
   b. You're at lunch with your boss at a fancy new restaurant. Your boss is very religious and does not approve of drinking during the workday. The waiter comes up to take your drink order.
   c. In the middle of your fifteenth run down the mountain, you try a different ski trail and discover a restaurant halfway down the slope. You're wet and cold and decide to stop for something to drink. Luckily, you find a comfortable chair by the fireplace.
   d. You're out drinking with friends from work on a Friday evening at your favorite bar.
   e. A friend is celebrating the birth of his first child with you and a few other people.
   f. The rainy weather in San Francisco surprises you one afternoon without your umbrella. You keep walking around in the drizzle, but after an hour, you're ready to sit down, dry off, and have something to drink. On Columbus Avenue, you find a great coffee shop and bookstore.

3. **Disappearing Dialog:** You have already practiced the conversation at the beginning of this unit. In groups of three, work with this conversation again, but this time one person looks at Edmundo's role in File 22, page 164; the second person looks at Rick's role in File 27, page 166; the third person looks at the waitperson's role in File 25, page 165. You will see your partners' complete conversations, but part of your conversation is missing. Be ready to help if your partners forget what to say. Anything appropriate is OK; it doesn't have to be the exact words.

4. **Crossword Puzzle:** With a colleague, fill in this crossword puzzle. Take turns giving each other clues. One person looks at File 31 on page 169. The second person looks at File 29 on page 168. At the end, check your answers with File 35, page 171.

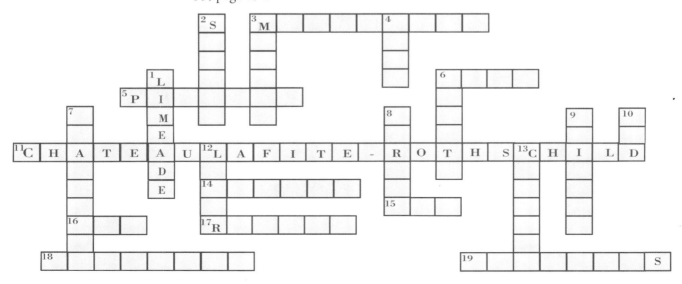

Unit 20

Etiquette in
Social Situations

 Listening Practice

A. Over lunch, Edmundo was thinking about some of the cross-cultural information that he heard about during a recent business communication seminar. Listen to Edmundo's conversation with Rick over lunch.

B. What do you remember from the conversation? Work with a small group and see how many points you can remember.

C. Listen again and check for points your group might have missed.

D. Edmundo's training materials included the social quiz below, showing social mistakes from the North American point of view. With a colleague, identify the social mistakes. Then see the explanation in File 33, page 170.

Can You Spot the Social Mistakes?

Listening Practice

A. **Listening for Speaker Attitude:** Listen to people talking about social behavior. Decide if the speaker's attitude is positive or negative.

Speaker Attitude		In My Country		
Positive	Negative	Perfectly Acceptable	A Little Unusual	Poor Manners
1. +	-	☐	☐	☐
2. +	-	☐	☐	☐
3. +	-	☐	☐	☐
4. +	-	☐	☐	☐
5. +	-	☐	☐	☐
6. +	-	☐	☐	☐
7. +	-	☐	☐	☐

B. The second time you listen, indicate how the behavior is viewed in your country. Then compare answers in pairs or small groups. There are no "right" answers here, but with varied national backgrounds in class, there will be different answers.

 ## Key Language

Listen, repeat, and practice aloud with a partner. Look at the statements made at a restaurant on the left and decide who might say them: the host, the guest, or either.

Social Niceties and Small Talk

Greetings
Hello! Good to see you.
How nice of you to join me [for lunch].
I'm afraid I can't stay long. I'm a little
   rushed.

Response
Nice to see you, too.
My pleasure.
No problem. I should make this quick,
   too.

Remarking on the Situation
You've picked out a great restaurant.
   This menu is fantastic!

Response
I'm glad you like it. They do have a
   good selection.

Starting a Topic of Conversation	**Response**
So what's going on at work these days? Any interesting projects?	We just signed a contract with Boeing. Everyone's excited about that.
Really? Tell me more about it.	Well, it's a long-term agreement . . .
Do you travel much for work?	Some. I've been to Asia twice this year.
What do you do in your free time?	I like tennis, and I play the guitar.
What about a game of golf this weekend?	I'm afraid I'm not much of a golfer.

Paying for Lunch	**Response**
Let me get that. (= pay for lunch or dinner)	Well, thank you. That's nice of you.

Ending the Conversation	**Response**
Thank you for lunch. It was great to see you.	I'm glad we had a chance to get together.
I've certainly enjoyed talking to you.	It's been great.
I'll hope to see you again soon.	Yes, I'll look forward to that.

Language Mastery

1. **Using Polite Language:** Change the wording of the following conversation so that the language is natural and polite. Use expressions from the Key Language sections. Then compare your changes with a colleague's. Finally, try both versions aloud several times to gain fluency.

   I'm inviting you for a drink after work.

   You want to go have a drink after work today?
   _____

   I accept.

   _____

   I want to go to Santiago's.

   _____

   The music is too loud there. I want to try the James Pub.

   _____

   OK, I suppose.

   _____

   I don't want to stay for long.

   _____

   Oh, well. I don't want to stay long either.

   _____

TOEIC Tip

Noncount Nouns	Count Nouns
meat, beef, poultry	But: hamburgers, steaks, fillets
tuna, shrimp, shellfish	lobsters, clams, oysters
luggage, baggage	bags, suitcases
equipment, machinery	tools, machines
money, currency, cash	dollars, "bucks," coins, quarters, dimes
information, intelligence	facts, statistics, data
correspondence, mail	letters, postcards, packages, e-mails
	pesos, riyals, pounds
	But no *-s:* won, yen, baht, dong

Notes:
1. Notice above how one word for something is countable but its synonym is noncount.
2. The Asian currencies won, yen, baht, ringgit, dong and renminbi are count nouns (*800,000 won*), but no plural *-s* ending is used.
3. Sometimes you will see a noncount noun used with *-s*. The meaning is "different types of," "different kinds of." This is a special use, not the usual use of noncount nouns.
   coffees = different kinds of coffee (e.g., from Colombia, Uruguay, and Hawaii)
   wines = dry, sweet, sparkling, red, white, rosé
   foods = different kinds of food (e.g., salads, pasta, breads, meats, vegetables)
4. To review more with noncount nouns, see the Language Notes, page 183.

2. Fill in the blanks with words from the TOEIC Tip.

   a. Do you get much _____ ? I usually get a lot of letters every day.

   b. All these heavy suitcases! How much _____ did you bring?

   c. How much office _____ should I order? I think we need several adding machines and two or three new computers.

   d. Do we have any _____ in the freezer? I was planning on making hamburgers tonight.

   e. What _____ do you have about the group coming to visit our company? Do you know when they're arriving or who is coming?

   f. I wonder what kinds of _____ they have at this restaurant. I'll ask for a wine list. They are sure to have many different kinds.

   g. How much _____ should I get for my trip to Japan?

Communication Activities

1. **Dinner Etiquette in Your Country:** Give a brief talk about dinner etiquette in your country to your class or in small groups. Prepare by thinking about these areas:

   • level of formality that is typical at a business meal
   • who sits down first, seating arrangements
   • what is important for the host to do during the meal
   • what conversation topics are avoided, if any
   • whether business is discussed before, after, during the meal or at all
   • who proposes a toast ("To your health!" "To our mutual success!")
   • who pays the bill

   Add any interesting cross-cultural information you can think of—especially if you know of something that is done differently in your culture. Try to cover as many of these areas as possible. Speak briefly, about three minutes. Leave time for questions.

2. **Dining Out:** Plan a social dinner with some local business people. You can make this dinner as simple or formal as you like. Work with your instructor to come up with a list of people to invite. They might be in business or native speakers of English. Try to get two guests for each small group of three or four from your class members.

   Work with your group to decide on the following.

   • A restaurant—where you can order in English
   • A convenient date and time for business people
   • What time to meet at the restaurant
   • The guests in your party
   • Transportation for the guests, if any
   • Who is going to make a reservation
   • Who is going to verify the location of the restaurant and write down directions for guests
   • Who is going to phone to invite the guests
   • Whether or not you are going to order wine, appetizers, or dessert
   • Who is going to think of a good toast
   • How you are going to pay in the restaurant
   • Who is going to pay

   Enjoy an evening out with your guests! Speak only in English. Be ready to share information about yourself and ask about your guests' professional interests, work, family, and so on. If discussions about politics or religion are too sensitive, avoid these areas.

   After the dinner, debrief together with your group by discussing these questions and anything else that comes up.

   a. Did you enjoy the dinner? What was the most enjoyable part?
   b. Did your guests have a pleasant evening? How do you know?
   c. What part was the most difficult?
   d. Do you have any suggestions to improve the success of your next dinner out?

Module 6

Discussing Issues

Unit 21

Starting a Discussion

Photo Credit: Tim Hancock

High-performance skiwear from Spyder . . .

The ultimate in function, comfort, and construction from the company that sponsors the U.S. Olympic Ski Racing Team. These are quality garments with exceptional protection and water repellency. Each comes with a lifetime warranty.

Look over the ad for Spyder skiwear. With a colleague, answer and discuss these questions.

1. Have you heard of this company? What is their claim to fame?
2. What image do you get of this skiwear? High quality? Medium quality? Low cost? What conveys this image?

> **the ultimate:** the best
> **garments:** clothes
> **warranty:** quality guarantee
> **claim to fame:** reason for being famous

Discussions

1. Assess your discussion skills.

	Excellent	Good	Needs Work
1. Introducing the topic of discussion	☐	☐	☐
2. Coming straight to the point	☐	☐	☐
3. Offering opinions or suggestions	☐	☐	☐
4. Agreeing or disagreeing politely	☐	☐	☐
5. Keeping focused on the topic	☐	☐	☐
6. Being persuasive; convincing others	☐	☐	☐
7. Winding up a discussion and stopping	☐	☐	☐

➤ In this module, focus on the areas that need the most work to see the greatest gain.

2. Choose the most polite, natural way to express the following ideas. Then discuss them with your instructor.

---

1. a. I need to talk to you.
   b. I wonder if you have a moment to talk.

2. a. I wonder if you could tell me about your products.
   b. I want to know about your products.

3. a. I'm not sure about that.
   b. I disagree.

4. a. I don't like our promotion policy.
   b. I have some questions about our promotion policy.

---

3. Why do people soften their language with expressions like *I wonder if . . . ?* When is it more effective to use this less direct language?

Listening Practice

Julie Nomura and Michael Ballard are U.S.-based buyers for Fuji Sports, a Japanese distributor of sports equipment and clothing. They are based in Aspen, Colorado. Ms. Nomura, a Japanese American, is the purchasing manager, and Michael, whose family has lived in Colorado for generations, is her assistant. They have been thinking about ordering skiwear from Spyder Active Sports, Inc., for Japanese consumers.

A. Listen and then answer the following questions.

1. Who starts the discussion?
2. What is the main point of the discussion?

B. Listen again and fill in the missing parts of the conversation. Then practice with a colleague.

Michael: Julie, _____ ? I wanted to talk with you about Spyder.

Julie: Sure. Let's go into my office. _____ ?

Michael: Well, Spyder's been making inroads with Japanese retailers—especially the high-end stores—ever since they started sponsoring Olympic ski racers. _____ to think seriously about carrying some of their lines.

Julie: Well, yeah. They seem eager to work with us. When's the rep coming?

Michael: Friday. Thomas Grant.

Julie: That's right. OK. You know, _____ the reaction of our Japanese manufacturers to more competing lines.

Michael: Everyone's got to compete in the global economy, don't you think? It's not as though anyone has exclusive rights with us. If we can get high quality at good prices, we need to go with it. _____ , Thomas Grant's been by once before. Remember him?

> **to make inroads:** to make good progress (in marketing a product)
> **to sponsor:** to support financially
> **don't you think?** don't you agree?
> **exclusive rights:** a relationship in which there is no competition, no third parties
> **to go with it:** to accept it, to agree to it

C. Discuss the following with a colleague.

1. What is Michael's first suggestion about Spyder lines? What reason does he give for this suggestion?
2. Does Michael seem like a practical person? Why or why not?
3. In this conversation, who asks the other person to come to the point right away?

Key Language

Listen, repeat, and practice aloud with a partner.

Starting a Discussion	Response
Have you got a moment?	Well, I have a big deadline today. How about tomorrow?
	I've got about five minutes. What's up?
	Sure, what's on your mind?
Would you have time for a discussion this week?	I'm out of town until Friday. Can it wait until next week?
	Friday's good for me. How about the afternoon—say 3:00?

❖ Which responses ask the speaker to come right to the point? Which sound most positive?

Leading into the Topic

I've been thinking a lot about our product promotion. (topic)

I wonder if we should create a new brochure with all our products. (main point)

We're making good sales on our website. (topic)

What we need now is more time to develop the website. (main point)

❖ Which statement of the main point sounds stronger?

Commenting on the Topic

Yes, we do need to talk about that. Maybe at our Friday meeting.

It's interesting that you bring that up. I've been thinking about it, too.

Discussion Format

Starting a Discussion	Have you got a moment?
Agreeing and Asking for the Topic	Sure. What's up?
Leading into the Topic	I've been thinking about Internet marketing.
Commenting on the Topic	Really? That's been on my mind, too.
Giving an Opinion	I think we should do more with our website.
Agreeing	Right. It would be great to have more visibility.
Asking for an Opinion	Well, what do you think about hiring a webmaster?

Language Mastery

1. Put the following sentences in order by writing 1 to 7 in the blanks to the left. Then write the function of each sentence in the blanks to the right. Choose from the following list of functions.

   - starting a discussion
   - getting to the main point
   - commenting on the topic
   - questioning the need
   - setting time limits and asking for the topic
   - disagreeing, giving reasons
   - leading into the topic

   a. __ Yeah, we should look at that. _____

   b. __ I've got 10 minutes before a _____

   meeting. What's up?

   c. __ I wonder if we need a _____

   commerce enabled website—

   order forms and everything.

   d. _1_ Have you got a moment? ___*Starting a discussion*___

e. __ Actually, millions of people

   buy from websites today.

   Security isn't an issue anymore.

   It's really no different than

   using a credit card in a store.

f. __ I've been thinking about

   developing our web sales.

g. __ People don't buy much on

   the web, do they?

Now practice the conversation with a colleague.

 2. **Catching Main Points:** You will hear six people talking. Write each person's main point on a separate piece of paper as you listen.

   Example: You will hear: I'd like to discuss our new products. We're not doing enough promotion for each product.

   You will write: ___more promotion of products___

3. **Starting Discussions:** Practice starting discussions. One person looks at File 34 on page 170; the second person looks at File 28 on page 167.

Professional Protocol

Global Cultures

Think about discussions in your own culture. Discuss these questions with a small group and compare customs in different countries. If your group is all of one nationality, see if you agree on the answers and compare your customs to the guidelines below for the United States.

1. Is it common to disagree? Is it ever important to disagree indirectly?
2. Is it more important in your country to finish a discussion or to get to a meeting on time and finish the discussion later?
3. Do people get to the point quickly, or do they like to give background information?

Guidelines for Discussions in the United States

- Time is a precious commodity. In discussions with Westerners, use people's time carefully. It will make it easier for them to work and do business with you.
- Prepare for important meetings and discussions. When you need to give information or try to persuade someone, decide in advance on the most important reasons, how to justify your points, which facts or statistics to use for a logical argument.
- Because of the sensitivity to time in U.S. culture, people respect time limits. If someone asks for "a moment," the discussion will be quick—only a few minutes. If more time is necessary, it is usual to set up a time to discuss the issue.

- In discussions with North Americans, be brief with small talk. Then get straight to the point. People in the United States usually do not have the patience to listen to a lot of background information, so give the least possible amount. They will ask you if they need more information.
- English has a lot of funny but negative expressions for being too talkative.

Unit 22

Giving Opinions, Agreeing, and Disagreeing

Michael Ballard has prepared some comparative pricing figures. He shows them to his boss, Julie Nomura, before the rep from Spyder arrives for his sales call. Read File 32 on page 169 to a colleague, who will fill in the prices below. Then listen as File 7 on page 155 is read to you for the rest of the prices. Check your answers together.

rep: sales representative

High-End Skiwear Pricing by Brand

Men's Skiwear

Spyder Quest .... $ _____
Expedition .... $ _____
Xpressions .... $ _____
Hot Dogger .... $ _____

Women's Skiwear

Spyder Picabo .... $ _____
Nuages .... $ _____
Xpressions .... $ _____
Blue Skies .... $ _____

Listening Practice

A. The following conversation between Julie and Michael takes place in Julie's office. Listen and then answer the questions.

1. When does Julie think Spyder skiwear became popular with Japanese consumers?
2. Does Julie think the Spyder lines will do well in Japan?
3. Who thinks Fuji Sports should buy in quantity?

B. Listen again and fill in the blanks. Then practice with a colleague.

➤ Read each line silently. Then look at your partner when speaking.

Michael:	So, Julie, _____ enough
	demand for this high-end skiwear?
Julie:	These lines really _____ .
	Remember? People were asking for Spyder, but it was only available
	in Tokyo. I think _____ .
Michael:	_____ . I
	think we should order in quantity and see if we can get a discount.
Julie:	_____ . Let's think about
	this a little more. You know, _____
	try a smaller order and see what happens.
Michael:	Really? Well, I suppose so. That's not as risky.

> **high end:** expensive and of high quality
> **in quantity:** a lot, in large amounts
> **risky:** (financially) dangerous

 Key Language

Listen, repeat, and practice aloud with a partner. Add your own examples.

Asking for Opinions
Do you think we should increase our marketing efforts?
What do you think about focusing on value to the customer?

Giving Opinions

Mild

⬆
⬇

Strong

I think we should focus on promotion efforts.
In my view, we should decide on some marketing priorities.
As far as I'm concerned, marketing really needs our attention.
I feel strongly that we should analyze the market.

Asking for Reasons	Responses
Why do you think that?	Because we need to increase sales.
What makes you say that?	Because our marketing budget is limited.

Agreeing	Disagreeing

Mild

Agreeing	Disagreeing
I think / guess / suppose so.	Do you really think so?
Yeah, that's right.	I'm not so sure about that.
Good point. I agree.	I see your point, but I'm just not sure that's
You bet. (= Yes!)	practical.
Absolutely.	Really? I don't think so.
I couldn't agree more.	That's out of the question. / That's impossible.

Strong

> *Notes:*
> 1. In Western business situations, people may disagree indirectly. They will say, "That's a good point but . . . ," before disagreeing.
> 2. In giving opinions, a frequent pattern is to give your opinion and ask right away what the other person's opinion is: "I think we should advertise in magazines. What do you think?"

Language Mastery

1. A. **Identifying Fact and Opinion.** Write *fact* (= something we can prove to be true) or *opinion* (= something a person thinks) for each sentence you hear.

   Examples: In my view, we should cancel this order.   _opinion_

   My boss canceled the order last Thursday.   _fact_

   1. _____   3. _____   5. _____   7. _____

   2. _____   4. _____   6. _____   8. _____

   B. **Understanding Tone of Voice.** Listen and decide whether the person expresses agreement or disagreement. The second time you listen, decide how strongly each person feels.

   Example: I'm not so sure about that.

   _____disagreement_____   ❏ strong   ❏ medium   ☑ mild

   1. _____   ❏ strong   ❏ medium   ❏ mild

   2. _____   ❏ strong   ❏ medium   ❏ mild

   3. _____   ❏ strong   ❏ medium   ❏ mild

   4. _____   ❏ strong   ❏ medium   ❏ mild

   5. _____   ❏ strong   ❏ medium   ❏ mild

   6. _____   ❏ strong   ❏ medium   ❏ mild

2. | Instructor Prep Note: Photocopy File 30 (enlarge, if possible) and cut the sentences into strips to pass out in order.

Sit in a circle in groups of 6 to 9. Your instructor will give each person one or two sentences from File 30, page 168. Study your sentence carefully so that you can say it perfectly without looking. The person with the first sentence begins by saying that sentence. The second person listens, paraphrases the first person's sentence and adds his or her own sentence. Continue until someone gives the entire story.

3. **Giving Opinions:** With a colleague, take turns discussing your opinions using the language in the list below. Discuss anything of current interest to you: good sources for job search information, the Internet, job opportunities in the twenty-first century, how to keep within a budget, how to increase sales, and so on. Your colleague will agree or disagree, give a reason, and then give an opinion with the next expression. Go through the list below twice.

    Example: A: As far as I'm concerned, company websites are the best way to look for a job. What do you think?

                    B: I agree. It's a good resource because companies give job openings online. I think companies should give more incentives to young employees.

    a. As far as I'm concerned . . .
    b. I think [managers] should . . .
    c. In my view, [the government] should . . .
    d. I feel strongly that . . .
    e. I'm really not so sure that [company] should . . .
    f. What do you think about . . . ?
    g. I suppose that [we] should . . .

4. **Leading a Discussion:** Form groups of three. Each person chooses a role (a, b, or c below). Read your role carefully and prepare to lead a short discussion on the topic. Follow this sequence.

    *   Restate the problem situation *briefly.*
    *   State your opinion and invite others' opinions.
    *   When people offer opinions, listen for their reasons. Ask for reasons if they are not given.
    *   When the topic is finished, invite the next discussion leader to begin.

    a. You are a salesperson. Your company has recently said that salespeople cannot give large gifts to clients because they may look like bribes. You're following company policy, but other salespeople still give large gifts to important customers. Your sales are falling. What should you do?

    b. You are an assistant manager. Your boss expects a lot of you and keeps giving you more and more responsibility. You feel good about the added responsibility, but there has been no increase in salary. With two young children, you could really use a raise. What should you do?

c. You're a manager. One person at work—the executive assistant for you and two other managers—is lazy. You're having trouble meeting deadlines because of this man's inefficiency. You have even seen him asleep at his desk. You aren't his supervisor, however. What should you do?

5. **Discussing Issues:**

A. Take time to think about a real problem situation you are familiar with. Form groups of three. Each person leads a short discussion on a real problem situation.

➤ The problem could be from your workplace or could be something in the news, for example. Make it something interesting to you and your audience. Decide who will be discussion leaders 1, 2, and 3.

B. During each discussion, listeners need to participate actively. *Listeners must complete two tasks per discussion. The discussion leader must continue talking until the listeners complete these tasks.*

Listener Tasks

Discussion 1: ❏ disagree politely with the discussion leader
               ❏ ask the discussion leader for a reason

Discussion 2: ❏ ask for clarification of a point
               ❏ request an example

Discussion 3: ❏ say something funny
               ❏ offer an opinion

Unit 23

Developing the Discussion

Thomas Grant, the rep from Spyder, is talking to Julie Nomura at Fuji Sports about Spyder skiwear products. Michael joins them briefly and then excuses himself to take care of other business. Thomas is trying to convince Julie that Japan will be a good market for Spyder's skiwear products. As a Japanese American with close ties to both countries, Julie is good at choosing product winners.

Digital Vision

Listening Practice

A. Fill in the blanks as you listen to this conversation between Julie and Thomas.

Thomas: It's great to see you again. How's business these days?

Julie: _____ , Thomas. Business

    is pretty good. The Japanese economy is doing well, so we're opti-

    mistic about this quarter. Last quarter wasn't our best.

Thomas: Hey, maybe what you need is some exciting new skiwear lines. You

    know, Japanese consumers see Spyder at every Winter Olympics. This

    stuff is hot! _____ in

    Japan because Japanese consumers want high quality, and these lines

    are exceptional.

Julie: Well, frankly, _____ .

    I'm a little hesitant, though. Spyder is largely untested in Japan.

    _____ they're expensive,

    and I don't want to have to discount my prices to retailers too much.

Thomas: OK. Well, there isn't really much risk to you as a distributor. We can

    handle your first purchase on a sale or return basis. If they don't sell,

    you can return them. Also, your customers can always return the

    item to the company for a refund. We've got a lifetime guarantee.

    _____ carry Spyder

    products. We want to make everything as easy as possible for you.

119

B. Without looking back to A, fill in the reasons given by Julie and Thomas as you listen again.

Julie: "We're optimistic about this quarter."

              Reason: _____

Julie: "I'm a little hesitant."

              Reason: _____

              Reason: _____

Thomas: "Well, there isn't really much risk to you as a distributor."

              Reason: _____

              Reason: _____

Key Language

Listen, repeat, and practice aloud with a partner. Where you see three dots (. . .), use Subject + Verb.

Developing the Discussion
In a discussion, you give reasons, offer opinions, and consider factors, as in these examples.

- This is especially important because . . . Another reason is that . . .
- I can think of two reasons: (a) we don't have enough staff, and (b) our staff isn't trained for these situations.
- This change will affect our bottom line. I also think it's risky because . . .
- One thing I'd like to stress is that . . . Another point is that . . . Still another point is that . . .
- As you may know, . . . A second consideration is that . . . In addition, . . .
- There are several factors. One is that . . . A second factor is that . . . And that's a third consideration.

Asking for Clarification
I'm sorry. I don't follow. (= I don't understand.) Could you go over that part again?
I didn't catch your second point.
Could you review that last point?
Could you give me an example? I'm not sure I follow.
Would you mind repeating what you just said (about pricing)?
Could you explain what you mean?

Clarifying
What I mean is that . . . (+ explanation)
What I'm saying is that . . . (+ explanation)
Let me put it this way. (+ explanation)

Language Mastery

1. With a colleague, make a list of several opinions. Then complete each of the following sentences developing the discussion with your opinions. Take turns.

   a. One thing I'd like to say is . . .
   b. Another important point for me is . . .
   c. I wonder if you could tell me . . . ?
   d. As you may know, . . .

   e. This is important because . . .
   f. Still another point is . . .
   g. I'd like to know . . .
   h. Could you tell me . . . ?

2. **Clarifying:** With a colleague, take turns asking for and providing clarification on the sentences below.

   Examples: *A:* My second point is that we simply don't have sufficient resources.
   B: Could you explain what you mean?
   A: What I'm saying is that we just don't have the people or the capital right now.

   B: I think we should take out a loan. We can pay back a loan over time.
   A: Would you mind going over what you just said about a loan?
   B: Not at all. What I mean to say is that we'll have more time to pay back a loan.

   a. A second factor is that it could increase product visibility for us.
   b. As you know, we have already shown them our capability.
   c. I can think of two reasons: we have the experience and our staff has the know-how.
   d. Well, we should do well because we produce several similar products.
   e. In addition, I'm just not sure we can meet their deadline.
   f. As you may know, our company has been active in this area for a decade or more.

3. **Adding a Point:** One person reads one of the following situations aloud. The other person agrees briefly (*Yes, True, Right, Good point*) and then adds a second point. Try each item two times, using different language to introduce the second point. Follow the example.

   Example: One thing I'd like to emphasize is that J&B salespeople have big territories. (They have a lot of different kinds of retail outlets to work with.)
   A: One thing I'd like to emphasize is that J&B salespeople have big territories.
   B: True, and another point is that they have a lot of different kinds of retail outlets to work with. OK, let's try it again. One thing I'd like to emphasize is that J&B salespeople have a lot of territory to cover.
   A: Good point. They also have a lot of different kinds of retail outlets to work with.

   a. Proctor & Gamble continues to be a very strong player. The company has so many different product lines. (It serves a lot of different markets worldwide.)
   b. Ben & Jerry's is a producer of high quality ice cream. They have a strong environmental program. (They have a program to support their local community.)

c. Johnson & Johnson is a huge company, but it has a lot of domestic competition. (There are many international companies that compete with Johnson & Johnson.)

d. Bausch & Lomb, the eye care products company, produces many items for contact lens wearers. (It makes prescription eyeglasses.)

f. Harry & David makes convenient fresh fruit gift packages. (It ships the packages anywhere.)

TOEIC Tip

Indirect Questions

Indirect questions are common in business and social interactions because they are more polite and less direct than regular questions. Compare the following.

Direct: How much is that going to cost?
Indirect: Could you tell me how much that's going to cost?

Introductory Phrase +	**Statement Word Order = Indirect Question**

Yes/No **Questions**

Could you tell me	if you have any contacts in Argentina?
I'd like to know	if I should go to Buenos Aires first or last.
Do you know	if the weather is warm there now?

Wh- **Questions**

Could you tell me	what contacts you have?
I was wondering	who I should talk to.
I wonder if you could tell me	what kind of gifts I should take.

Note: Use a question mark only when the introductory phrase has question word order: Could you tell me . . . ?

4. **Using Indirect Language:** Practice using indirect language in pairs. One person looks at File 26 on page 166. The other person looks at File 23 on page 164.

5. **Using Polite Language:** Rewrite these sentences in a more polite and less direct way. Go over answers out loud with a colleague.

Example: I want some tickets to the football game.

   I wonder if it's possible to get tickets to the game.

a. That is out of the question. We can't travel during the busy summer season.

_____

b. I want the names of your contacts in Malaysia.

_____

c. What is your company's annual revenue?

_____

d. What time does the train to Boston leave?

_____

e. What will my raise for next year be?

_____

f. My boss wants to stay at your condo in Cancun.

_____

g. I want to talk to you.

_____

Unit 24

Summarizing Views and Making Suggestions

Michael is asking about Julie's meeting with Thomas Grant. Michael takes notes as Julie tells him about the meeting.

 Listening Practice

A. Listen to the conversation between Julie and Michael. Fill in the missing parts in Michael's notes.

Fuji Sports

Spyder Ski Wear

Followup

Spyder, Inc.
Thomas Grant
Sales Representative
303/555-2505

Order _____ Picabo & Quest

Ask about _____

Request _____ for retailers

Request _____

B. Listen again and answer these questions.

1. What kind of risk is involved in placing this order?
2. What does Julie think about Spyder products?
3. What is Julie's concern about the lifetime guarantee?
4. What is the last thing she asks Michael to do?

C. Now practice the following conversation with a colleague. Try both parts several times.

Michael:	So how did the meeting go?
Julie:	I had a good discussion with Thomas.
Michael:	Yeah? What did he have to say?
Julie:	Well, for one thing, he told me that we could place our first order sale or return. Pretty nice—no risk to us.
Michael:	That's great. So you feel confident about placing an order?
Julie:	I really do. Thomas answered all my questions, and I feel great about Spyder products. He told me something about their lifetime guarantee too, but I can't remember who customers return the product to—the retailer or the company. We should also ask him for some brochures for our retailers.
Michael:	So you want me to ask him about the lifetime guarantee and about getting some brochures when I place an order?
Julie:	That would be great, Michael. Uh, let's get about 100 of both styles.
Michael:	OK, I'll get our usual numbers of small, medium, large, and extra large. Uh, that's Picabo and Quest, right?
Julie:	Yeah. We liked those two styles best. And why don't you see if we can get them delivered to the warehouse before my trip to Japan next month?

brochures: informational papers to pass out to possible clients
styles: the designs of clothes

 ## Key Language

Listen, repeat, and practice aloud with a partner. Add your own examples of suggestions.

Making Suggestions	**Response**	**Positive**
Why don't we discuss this awhile?	→ Sure. Sounds great.	↑
Why don't you tell the boss your plan?	→ Yeah, good idea.	
Let's ask for some time off.	→ OK	
I think we should fax it immediately.	→ OK, but I'm not sure about this.	
How about faxing the boss this information?	→ Do you really think we should?	
Should we talk to the director?	→ I don't think so.	
Maybe we should call him at home.	→ I can't support doing that.	↓
		Negative

Write three suggestions for a colleague. Then discuss together.

_____

_____

_____

Summarizing Views	**Response**
So you feel confident about ordering?	I really do.
So you [don't] think we should place an order?	Right.
That's Picabo and Quest, right?	You got it. (= You understand correctly.)
OK, so where do we stand on this?	We're waiting to hear from them.
So how do you feel about Proctor & Gamble?	I would like to work with them.
So what did you decide about marketing?	We need to be more systematic.
OK, I'll finish the proposal, fax it, and wait to hear.	Good.

Language Mastery

1. Practice making suggestions for a colleague to respond to. After you both finish writing, take turns going through your lists out loud and responding.

    a. Why don't we _____ ?

    b. So how do you feel about _____ ?

    c. So what did you decide about _____ ?

    d. Should we _____ ?

    e. How about _____ ?

    f. I think maybe we should _____ .

2. **Summarizing:** Listen to the following views. You will hear each one twice. Write questions that restate the speakers' points. Then listen again and compare answers.

    Example: There are many ways to help low-income people. One way is for private-sector businesses to provide jobs.

    So you think the private sector should try to help with this problem?

    a. _____

    b. _____

    c. _____

    d. _____

3. **Disappearing Dialog:** You have already practiced the conversation at the beginning of this unit. Work with this conversation again but this time one person looks at Julie's role in File 21, page 163, and the second person looks at Michael's role in File 18, page 161. You will see your partner's complete conversation, but part of your conversation is missing. Be ready to help if your colleague forgets what to say next.

4. **Structured Discussion:** Have a discussion with a colleague using the model below. When you finish, try one or two similar conversations with your own topics.

Start				
Do you have a moment?		Actually, I liked your frankness. I think I should try to be more critical, too.	So I should be perfectly frank in this report?	That's right. I think we all should.
Sure. What's up?	Well, I wanted to ask you about that report.	Was I too critical?		Well, I'm glad to hear that. In fact, I couldn't agree more.
				As far as I'm concerned, it does us more good to be honest than to gloss over the problem.
Well, I'm not too eager to get fired. Why don't you talk to him?	Sure. Why not? The worst he can do is fire us.	Me too. So you feel like we can take this to the boss?	Let's talk to the boss about this. I think it's important.	You bet. And another point is that we can show the real problems are not caused by our department.
Finish				

5. **Summarizing Views:** Take a few minutes to write down some questions to ask people. Use your knowledge of colleagues' likes, dislikes, and opinions to ask about topics that are important to them. After someone answers one of your questions, make a follow-up comment or suggestion.

Example: *A:* Cristina, what do you think about increasing taxes on cigarettes for medical research?

B: I'm against it. I smoke, you know.

A: Yes, I know. But don't you think people who smoke should pay for the costs of smoking?

Communication Activities

1. **Problem Solving**

   A. Begin by working individually. Think of a problem in business or personal life. It can be real or imaginary, or you can use one of the following examples.

      My boss gives all the good assignments to my colleagues.
      I feel like I'm wasting time during my daily commute.
      I have a difficult time making decisions.
      My husband/wife is talking about an expensive vacation that I don't think
        we can afford.
      My brother is flunking out of graduate school.

   B. Then, in small groups, follow this sequence.

      • One person quickly describes a problem.
      • A second person, the problem solver, asks questions to get more information.
          Why is that? Why do you think that happened?
          How do you know that? Could you explain that a little more?
          The problem solver also makes several suggestions to solve the problem.
            Maybe you should . . . (+ V). Have you tried . . . (+ V-*ing*)?
      • The rest of the group listens and acts as observers. After the person with the problem and the problem solver finish talking, the observers then summarize the conversation.

   C. Each group decides on one example to summarize again for the entire class.

2. **Discussing Issues.** Prepare to lead a discussion group. Follow these steps.

   a. Read a current business newspaper or magazine and find a short article. Make sure that the article will be interesting to colleagues and that it expresses opinion. (Find current articles of opinion to choose from at the website http://www.bizenglish.com if you have Internet access.)
   b. Read the article carefully. Ask your instructor about difficult expressions. (Online articles have definitions for difficult vocabulary and business slang.)
   c. Prepare to lead a discussion on the topic of your article. Each person in your group will give a small amount of background information. Then tell two or three main points. Give your opinion about some aspect of the article. Ask for members' opinions. If the article brings up a problem, ask members for suggestions and react to the suggestions given being careful to use polite language.
   d. In groups, take turns leading a discussion. When someone else is leading the discussion, pay close attention so that you can offer your opinions and suggestions.

3. **Discussing a Product Launch**

   A. In small groups, discuss how to launch a product. First discuss and decide the following.

      • What company your group wants to represent—your choice!
      • What kind of product or service you are launching—anything you want!
      • Roles for each member of your group: CEO, marketing manager, finance manager, advertising manager, human resources manager

B. After the discussion with group members, prepare for your role. Check your file.

CEO:	File 14	page 159
Marketing Manager:	File 11	page 157
Finance Manager:	File 6	page 154
Advertising Manager:	File 4	page 153
Human Resources Manager:	File 2	page 151

C. Discuss your product launch including all members in the discussion. Work out as many of the details as possible. Your CEO will run the meeting and will begin by asking what items to put on the meeting agenda. Be sure to get your issues on the agenda.

Listening Script
and Answer Key

Module 1

Unit 1. Introducing Yourself

Listening Practice (page 3)

A. Hi, I'm Richard Carmichael. I work for the California Department of Transportation—CalTrans—where I'm chief of planning. I'm here in Paris on a fact-finding mission. I want to get information about the high-speed trains made in France for possible use in California. I'm going to meet with representatives of a French company that makes high-speed trains. My e-mail address is <carmichael@caltrans.org>.

I'm Nicole Legrand. It's nice to meet you. I work for a French train company called TVE International. I'm a manager in sales and marketing. I usually work with our international clients, and I'll be meeting with Mr. Carmichael soon to discuss our trains. My sister knows Mr. Carmichael and referred him to our company. As it turns out, Mr. Carmichael may do business with us. Let me give you my e-mail address. It's <legrand@tve.co.fr>.

Listening Practice (page 4)

A. *Carmichael:* Hello, Ms. Legrand?
    Legrand: <u>You must be Mr. Carmichael.</u> I'm pleased to meet you.
    Carmichael: I'm <u>glad to meet you,</u> too.
    Legrand: Welcome to Paris, Mr. Carmichael. <u>How was your flight?</u>
    Carmichael: Fine. A little long, but fine.
    Legrand: Well, let's go get your bags, and then I'll take you to your hotel. <u>You must be tired.</u>
    Carmichael: Thank you. Yes, I guess I am a little tired.

Language Mastery (page 5)

1. a. Hello. My name's Jeff Smith.
    b. I'm Linda Jackson. Glad to meet you.
    c. I don't believe we've met. I'm George Winters.
    d. How do you do? My name's Mary Jenkins.
    e. Michael Wentworth. Good to meet you.
    f. Hello. I'm Nick Brunner.
    g. Hi, I'm Nancy.
    h. Nice to see you. My name's Bill.

Unit 2. Introducing Others

Listening Practice (page 7)

A. *Legrand:* Mr. Carmichael, I'd like you to meet Georges Bernard, TVE's managing director. Mr. Bernard, this is Richard Carmichael from the California Department of Transportation.

Carmichael:	How do you do, Mr. Bernard?
Bernard:	How do you do? It's a pleasure to meet you, Mr. Carmichael.
Carmichael:	It's good to meet you too. I'm very happy to be here.
Legrand:	As chief of planning, Mr. Carmichael has been working on the San Francisco to L.A. high-speed train project.
Bernard:	Yes, I'm looking forward to discussing your project. I think you'll be impressed with our new models. Where do you live in California?
Carmichael:	San Francisco. Moved there from San Diego six years ago.
Legrand:	OK, well, I'll give you two a chance to get acquainted. By the way, Mr. Bernard, you'll be happy to know that Mr. Carmichael is quite a golfer! My sister and her husband play frequently with Mr. Carmichael and his wife.
Bernard:	Really?

Language Mastery (page 8)

1. a. I'm Alex Smith, sales representative for Allied Distribution, Incorporated. My phone number isn't on the business card. It's area code (213) 555-9722.

    b. I just met John Edward Applegate. He's the CEO for Applegate Enterprises in Baltimore, Maryland. He asked me to give you his card.

    c. Hello, my name's Roberta Henderson. I'm senior vice president of Elgin Corporation in Boston, Massachusetts. I wanted to ask you about something if you have a moment.

    d. When you're in Colorado, I want you to meet Patricia Bartlett. She's the director of public relations for Colorado Savings and Loan. Her branch office is located in Colorado Springs.

3. a. I'm so glad to meet you.

    b. How do you do? I'm Bob Johnson.

    c. I'd like you to meet George Sanders, our director of marketing.

    d. It's a pleasure to meet you.

    e. Let me give you my business card.

    f. How was your flight?

Unit 3. Starting a Conversation

Listening Practice (page 11)

A. | | |
|---|---|
| *Legrand:* | <u>So, tell me,</u> Mr. Carmichael, have you ever been to Paris before? |
| *Carmichael:* | Yes, fifteen years ago as a student. <u>By the way,</u> please call me Richard. |
| *Legrand:* | Sure—<u>if you'll call</u> me Nicole. What were you studying? |
| *Carmichael:* | Well, I was studying architecture. After I went back to California, I changed my major to transportation engineering. |
| *Legrand:* | More practical? |
| *Carmichael:* | <u>That's right.</u> And better employment opportunities. |
| *Legrand:* | How long have you worked at CalTrans? |
| *Carmichael:* | <u>Well, let's see,</u> I've been there nine years now. It's interesting, and I like the people I work with. How long have you been with TVE? |

C. 1. So, tell me
    2. By the way
    3. Well, let's see

Language Mastery (page 12)

1. | | |
|---|---|
| *Rachel Petersen:* | It's good to meet you. <u>So where are you from?</u> |
| *Don Baxter* | It's nice to meet someone from your part of the world. <u>What line of business are you in?</u> |
| *David Thompson:* | I'm glad to meet you. <u>So, how long are you here for?</u> |

2. a. My drive to work is quite long.
    b. This place makes me think of my last vacation.
    c. My company sent me to Korea last year.
    d. My work keeps me very busy.
    e. I work at a bank locally.
    f. I'm from New York.
    g. I got my degree several years ago.
    h. I studied business in the United States.

5. Ever been to Vancouver?
    Yeah. A couple of times. How 'bout you?
    Last year I was there for a conference.
    I bet you saw the old town area when you were there, didn't you?
    Yeah, it's a beautiful city, isn't it?

Unit 4. Ending a Conversation and Leave-taking

Listening Practice (page 15)

A. *Nicole:*   Well, <u>it's really been good</u> to have a chance to talk with you in more detail. Unfortunately, I <u>need to get back</u> to the office for a 2:00 appointment.

   Richard: No problem. Let's see. I'll walk back with you—I'm going to tour the production facility. I'm interested in seeing exactly what these trains look like.

[Back at TVE headquarters]

   Nicole: <u>It's been a pleasure,</u> Richard. I'll introduce you to Robert Cartier, and he'll take you over to the production facility and show you around.

   Richard: You've been so helpful. <u>I appreciate</u> all the information you've given me. I'm looking forward to the tour.

   Nicole: Yes. I hope you enjoy it. . . . Ah, Richard, let me introduce Robert Cartier, our public relations manager. Robert, this is Richard Carmichael from the California Department of Transportation.

   Richard: How do you do, Mr. Cartier? Pleased to meet you.

   Robert: How do you do, Mr. Carmichael? My pleasure.

   Nicole: Richard's ready to see the production facility now. I'll see you both tomorrow. <u>Will you excuse me?</u>

   Richard: Sure. See you tomorrow, Nicole. And <u>thanks for lunch.</u>

C. Unfortunately I need to get back to the office for a 2:00 appointment. / It's been a pleasure, Richard. / Will you excuse me?

Language Mastery (page 17)

1. Conversation 1. That's a great idea. Let's think about it more. <u>Well, I've got to get ready for a meeting.</u>
    Conversation 2. I'm sure <u>you have a lot of work to do.</u> Maybe we can continue our discussion in a few days.
    Conversation 3. I sure would enjoy working with you on this. It sounds like an interesting project. <u>Oh—it's getting quite late. I didn't realize the time.</u>
    Conversation 4. <u>Well, I think we're ready to start work on this project now.</u> I won't take any more of your time.

Module 2

Unit 5. Talking about Facts and Figures

Listening Practice (page 22)

A. 1. Mexico is expected to have a population of <u>98</u> million people next year.
    2. This year, gross domestic product (GDP) grew at a rate of <u>4.3</u> percent.
    3. This year, Mexico's exports amounted to U.S.$<u>106</u> billion.
    4. Imports totaled U.S.$<u>102.7</u> billion, leaving a trade surplus of approximately U.S.$<u>3.2</u> billion.
    5. After falling to <u>26.5 percent</u> last year, inflation in Mexico is expected to drop further to <u>17.5 percent</u> by the end of this year.
    6. The peso has appreciated modestly this year, yielding an exchange rate of around <u>7.85</u> to the U.S. dollar.

B. 1. f   2. e   3. d   4. a   5. b   6. g   7. c

		True	False
C. 1.	Mexico exports more goods to Japan than to the United States.		☑
2.	Exports to Spain account for more than exports to Japan.		☑
3.	Mexico exports more goods to the United States than to any other country.	☑	
4.	Exports to other countries account for more than exports to Spain and Japan combined.	☑	

Listening Practice (page 24)

1. a. January 5, 1972
    b. December 23, 1908
    c. March 13, 1845
    d. October 4, 2005
    e. November 19, 2014
    f. August 2, 1637

2. a. 1,469
    b. 9,728,350
    c. 17,614,540
    d. 313
    e. 597,415
    f. 2,360,417,316

3. a. 5.75
    b. 2 1/3
    c. 6 3/4
    d. 5 7/8
    e. 9.876
    f. 8 1/2

Language Mastery (page 27)

3. 1. 15 (b)
    2. 80,000 (c)
    3. 30 (b)
    4. 240 (b)
    5. 554 (c)
    6. 3,221 (a)
    7. 4,798,301 (c)

4. Good evening. This is the NRW nightly financial news for Thursday, November 13th. The Dow Jones closed at 7,487.76, up 86.44 points; the NASDAQ closed at 1,557.74, up 16.02 points; and the Standard & Poor's 500 closed at 916.66, edging up 7.85 points. Now let's look at some blue chip stocks. IBM closed at 107 3/16, up 1/16. General Electric finished at 76 1/4, up 2 11/16. Microsoft closed at 130 1/2, up 1 15/16. Exxon ended the day at 59 9/16, down 3/8, and finally, GM closed at 59 1/2, up 2 3/4.

Thursday, November 13

Dow Jones Industrial Average	The NASDAQ Composite	Standard & Poor's 500
Closed at: 7487.76	Closed at: 1557.74	Closed at: 916.66
↑ 86.44	↑ 16.02	↑ 7.85

	IBM	General Electric	Microsoft	Exxon	GM
	107³⁄₁₆ +¹⁄₁₆	76¼ +2¹¹⁄₁₆	130½ +1¹⁵⁄₁₆	59⁹⁄₁₆ -³⁄₈	59½ +2¾

Unit 6. Introducing Your Company

Listening Practice (page 29)

A. Ceramex was founded in 1967 by Roberto Martinez in northern Mexico. Ceramex manufactures ceramic floor and wall tile to satisfy the domestic and export markets. Because of the artistic designs and high quality of its products, Ceramex is recognized as one of the leading producers of ceramic tile in the world. Ceramex has seven factories in northern Mexico and employs 750 people. At present, Ceramex has increased its production capacity by opening two new factories. It acquired a U.S. subsidiary in 1990. Sixty percent of Ceramex's products are sold domestically; 25 percent are exported to the United States, 10 percent to Canada, and 5 percent to countries in South America.

Unit 7. Describing Company Organization

Listening Practice (page 34)

A. Now I'd like to talk about the organization of Ceramex. As you can see from the chart, at the top we have the CEO who is in charge of the general direction of the company. From there our company is divided into four main areas: Marketing and Sales, Finance, Production, and Human Resources. Although they work closely together, Marketing and Sales is divided into two departments: Marketing and Sales. The Sales Department then has two separate areas: domestic and international sales. If you look at the chart, you can see that Production is divided into four departments: Design, Manufacturing, Quality Assurance, and Purchasing.

Language Mastery (page 36)

2. We have some of the most qualified people in the country in our top management positions. Andrew P. Thompson is president and CEO. Under Andrew, we have Phyllis Jensen, executive vice president and COO, Ronald H. Calder, director of sales and marketing, and Brian Jacobson as chief financial officer. Our director of technology development is Susan Philips, Harold Smith is general manager of technology manufacturing, and Adrienne Chin is director of information technology.

Unit 8. Describing Job Responsibilities

Listening Practice (page 38)

A. *Susan Peterson:*   I certainly enjoyed hearing about your company, Manuel. How long have you been at Ceramex?

Manuel Sanchez: I joined the company about fifteen years ago, and I've been in marketing and sales for the past seven years.

Susan Peterson: So what exactly do you do?

Manuel Sanchez: I'm responsible for international sales and marketing. I supervise a staff of twelve people, and I oversee all international sales and distribution agreements.

Susan Peterson: That must keep you busy, and you must travel a lot.

Manuel Sanchez: I sure do. In fact, I'm on the road about fifty percent of the time.

Susan Peterson: Sounds like fun to me. Well, I want you to know that we're very impressed with Ceramex, and we are looking forward to working with you.

	True	False
1. Manuel has been at Ceramex for seven years.		☑
2. He is now in marketing and sales.	☑	
3. He supervises a staff of twenty people.		☑
4. He travels about 80 percent of the time for his job.		☑

Language Mastery (page 39)

1. John Roberts works for Lockheed. He is responsible for research and development of satellite systems. Sara Burton works for American Express Corporation. She is in charge of South American Operations. Max Smith works for Arthur Anderson Consulting. He heads the legal department and oversees all contracts.

4. Of course two days are never the same. But on a typical day, I get to my office at about 8:30. I tend to drink a cup of coffee while I open my mail. After I sort through my mail and my in box, I prioritize my activities for the day. I usually get a lot of letters from clients in the United States, so then I dictate letters to my secretary. She is bilingual, so I feel confident about the quality of the English. Then around 11:00 I attend a planning meeting with my sales staff. At that meeting we deal with urgent items and talk about our short- and long-term sales strategies.

    I often have lunch meetings with clients, and they usually last one and a half to two hours. This kind of entertaining is very important in sales. It helps to solidify relationships. After lunch, I do a lot of telephoning. I have clients and distributors in Mexico, the United States, and Brazil. This can take from one to two hours. After telephoning, I get on the computer and look at our orders, sales projections, and inventory. Then I answer my e-mail.

    On Fridays at 4:00, if I am not out of town, I attend a meeting with the director of marketing. He usually expects a report of weekly activities, and we discuss sales incentives and strategies. At about 5:00 I check with my secretary to confirm my schedule and appointments for the following day. By the time I wrap everything up, it's usually about 7:00. I'm often the last person to leave the office.

Module 3

Unit 9. Problems Telephoning

Listening Practice (page 46)

A. *Jack Lee:*   I've been trying to reach Peter Miller of Microproducts for the past hour. You won't believe the problems I've had.

Susan Potter:	Really? What happened?	
Jack Lee:	Well first I tried four or five times, and the line was busy. Then I finally got through, but the receptionist put me on hold.	
Susan Potter:	For how long?	
Jack Lee:	For about ten minutes. Of course, I hung up. Then I tried again. This time I told the receptionist to put me through to Peter directly. But you'll never guess what happened.	
Susan Potter:	What?	
Jack Lee:	I got disconnected while she was transferring me. You know, I'm getting fed up with this! There are plenty of other suppliers around.	

		True	False
B. 1.	He tried to call Peter Miller at MCI.		☑
2.	The first four times he called, the line was busy.	☑	
3.	When he got through, the receptionist put him on hold.	☑	
4.	He was on hold for two or three minutes.		☑
5.	When he called the second time he was able to speak to Peter Miller.		☑
6.	Jack is considering using another supplier.	☑	

Unit 10. Making a Phone Call

Listening Practice (page 49)

A. *Receptionist:*	Good morning, Global Telecom. <u>May I help you?</u>	
Jung:	Good morning. I'd <u>like to speak to</u> Jack Lee in purchasing, please.	
Receptionist:	May I <u>tell him who's calling?</u>	
Jung:	Yes, <u>this is</u> Sung-Wook Jung of SRG Electronics in Korea. I'm calling to talk about our telecommunications equipment.	
Receptionist:	One moment <u>and I'll transfer</u> your call.	

Language Mastery (page 51)

2. a. (617) 495-3216
   b. (303) 463-1928
   c. 1-800-579-3000
   d. (212) 256-9874
   e. (415) 531-7652
   f. (305) 777-5411

3. a. "Hello, <u>John.</u> This is <u>Irene Jenkins.</u> I'm calling to <u>remind</u> you of our <u>appointment</u> next <u>Tuesday</u> at <u>2:30.</u> I'll see you then."
   b. "Hi. This is <u>Tracy.</u> Sorry I'm <u>late.</u> I got <u>stuck</u> in rush hour <u>traffic.</u> I should be there in about <u>30 minutes.</u> See you."

4. Call 1.   May I say who's calling?
                   Yes. This is David Edwards of Tech Solutions calling for Peter Wilkinson.
   Call 2.   Hello. This is Kathy Thompson of Hewlett Packard. I'd like to speak to Melissa Anderson, please.
   Call 3.   Good morning. This is Helen Marks of the Environmental Protection Agency. May I please speak to Bill Clemson?

5. a.

Receptionist:	Good morning, Edwards & Sons. May I help you?	
Janice Peterson:	Good morning. I'd like to speak to Fred Jones, please.	
Receptionist:	I'm afraid he's in a meeting at the moment. Would you like to leave a message?	
Janice Peterson:	Yes. Please ask him to call Janice Peterson at General Electric when he's free. I'm calling to get a current price list.	
Receptionist:	Does he have your number, Ms. Peterson?	

Janice Peterson:	I don't think so. My number is (415) 938-2715.
Receptionist:	That's (415) 938-2715?
Janice Peterson:	That's right.
Receptionist:	Okay. I'll give him the message.

b.
Receptionist:	Good morning, Edwards & Sons. May I help you?
Ted Martin:	Yes. This is Ted Martin calling from Pacific Shipping. I'd like to speak to Margaret Smith, please.
Receptionist:	I'm sorry, Ms. Smith is out of town today. Can someone else help you?
Ted Martin:	Um . . . this isn't urgent. Please have her give me a call when she gets back. I'd like to set up an appointment.
Receptionist:	What's your number, Mr. Martin?
Ted Martin:	It's (516) 224-7800.
Receptionist:	That's (516) 224-7800?
Ted Martin:	That's correct.
Receptionist:	I'll give her the message, Mr. Martin.

Unit 11. Scheduling a Meeting

Listening Practice (page 54)

A.
Lee:	Hello, Mr. Jung. Jack Lee speaking.
Jung:	Hello, Mr. Lee. I'm with SRG Electronics. and I was hoping to talk to you about our line of electronic parts.
Lee:	Oh, yes, I've heard of SRG. How are things going in Korea?
Jung:	Good, thanks. In fact, recently there's been a lot of demand for our parts, so we've been very busy.
Lee:	Glad to hear that. I'd certainly be interested in your prices.
Jung:	Well, it just so happens I'm going to be in San Francisco next week. I was wondering if you'd have time to get together.
Lee:	You bet. When will you be here?
Jung:	Next Wednesday and Thursday. What does your schedule look like?
Lee:	Um . . . Let me check my calendar. (after a few moments) Let's see, I have a meeting on Wednesday morning. How about Wednesday afternoon at about two o'clock?
Jung:	Two o'clock is fine.

Language Mastery (page 56)

1. a. "Good morning, <u>Dorothy.</u> This is <u>Claudia Bransford.</u> I'm afraid I have to <u>cancel</u> our meeting today. My <u>daughter</u> is <u>sick</u> with the flu. I'll give you a <u>call</u> in a <u>few days</u> to <u>reschedule.</u> I'm <u>terribly sorry</u> about this."

   b. "Hello, <u>Jim.</u> This is <u>Bill Sherman</u> at <u>Merrill Lynch.</u> Give me a <u>call</u> as soon as possible. I've got some <u>news</u> about a <u>stock offering.</u> My number is <u>483-8000.</u>"

2. Call 1.
Susan Potter:	Good morning, Global Telecom. Susan Potter speaking.
Ross Wilson:	Good morning, Susan. This is Ross Wilson. How are you doing?
Susan Potter:	Great. How about you?
Ross Wilson:	I'm doing fine. Listen, I wanted to set up a time to show you our new copier. It's really fantastic.
Susan Potter:	Okay. Um . . . I'm really busy this week, but next week is good.
Ross Wilson:	How about Thursday morning at 9:00? Is that too early?
Susan Potter:	No, not at all. Do you want me to come to your demo office, or can you bring the copier here?
Ross Wilson:	I can bring it to your office.
Susan Potter:	Great. I'll look forward to seeing you next Thursday, bright and early, at my office.

Call 2.

Susan Potter:	Good afternoon, Global Telecom. This is Susan Potter.
Angela Jones:	Hello, Susan. This is Angela Jones.
Susan Potter:	Hi, Angela. How's it going?
Angela Jones:	Good, thanks. I'm calling because I have to change our lunch meeting. An important client is coming into town next Wednesday.
Susan Potter:	No problem. Shall we reschedule?
Angela Jones:	Sure. How about in a couple of weeks, say April 21st?
Susan Potter:	Let's see, that's a Tuesday, right?
Angela Jones:	Yeah.
Susan Potter:	That's a good day for me. Shall we meet at the Thai Garden Restaurant at noon?
Angela Jones:	Sounds good. That's one of my favorite restaurants. And gee, I'm really sorry about next Wednesday.
Susan Potter:	It's no problem, really. I'll see you on Tuesday, April 21st.

demo: a demonstration
to reschedule: to schedule at another time

5.   1. Q: When will the meeting be over?
      (A.) I have no idea. It should have ended by now.
      B. I'll be meeting with them tomorrow.
      C. I'll call him as soon as the meeting is finished.

    2. Q: Can I get a ride home with you today? My car is in the shop.
      A. Yes, I'm riding the bus home today.
      B. Sure, I'd like to go shopping.
      (C.) No problem. Meet me in the parking lot after work.

    3. Q: How about lunch next week when you're in town?
      A. Sure, I'll be in town next week.
      (B.) Unfortunately, I'm booked every day. What about dinner?
      C. I'd love to get together for golf next week.

    4. Q: Is Susan Jacobs in, please?
      A. Thank you for calling, I'll give her the message.
      B. Good morning, Mr. Phillips. How may I help you?
      (C.) I'm sorry. Susan is away from her desk. Would you like to leave a message?

    5. Q: Who can I get to type this proposal?
      A. Take the proposal with you to the meeting.
      (B.) Try asking Jim. He might have time.
      C. I really need the proposal by tomorrow!

    6. Q: Henry, how about lunch?
      (A.) I'd love to, but I'm swamped. How about tomorrow?
      B. Let's get some lunch.
      C. Sure. Why don't we have lunch today?

    7. Q: Would you mind going over the terms of the contract with me?
      A. Yes. Which points are you worried about?
      B. Sure. I'd be happy to.
      (C.) Not at all. Let's start with number one.

    8. Q: Are you going to Seattle next week?
      (A.) It depends on whether I can get someone to cover for me here.
      B. Seattle is a great place for a conference.
      C. Yes, I've been to Seattle several times.

Unit 12. Ending a Phone Conversation

Listening Practice (page 59)

A. *Lee:*   Shall we meet at my office?

    Jung: Yes, that's a good idea. Where are you located?

    Lee: We're at 555 California, Suite 790.

    Jung: Uh, I'm sorry, could you repeat that?

    Lee: Sure. It's 555 California Street, Suite 790. In the financial district.

    Jung: Oh, I'm staying at the Marriott on Market Street, so that should be easy to find. So, we'll meet at two o'clock next Wednesday at your office. And you're at 555 California Street?

    Lee: That's right. Suite 790. Just go out of the hotel and turn right on Market. Go about six blocks. Then turn left on California. Go up the street about five blocks. Our building is on your left. You can't miss it.

    Jung: That sounds easy enough. Well, I'll let you get back to work. Nice talking to you.

    Lee: Yes, and I'm looking forward to meeting you. See you next week. Good-bye.

Answers: 1. T   2. F   3. T   4. F   5. F

Language Mastery (page 62)

1.   a. (male voice) . . . I agree. We need to look at expanding into Europe as well as Asia. Listen, I've got to look over my notes before the sales meeting. Let's talk about this more tomorrow.

    b. (female voice) . . . And I'm sure we'll get the go-ahead to place an order soon. Well, I've got another call coming in. I'm glad I had a chance to talk with you.

    c. (male voice) . . . I think we'll be making a decision on a contractor soon. Well, I've got to get going. I have a lunch appointment in a few minutes. Good talking to you.

Module 4

Unit 13. Making Plans

Listening Practice (page 68)

A. *Wang:*   As you know, we'll be exhibiting at the World PC Expo in Japan in November, but we need to make plans for one other international trade show next year.

    Fong: Well, what're our budget constraints?

    Wang: Unfortunately, this is a tight year for us, so we can do the Japanese show and one other big show. I sent you files about the Las Vegas Consumer Electronics Show and the COMDEX show in London. So, what do you think?

    Lee: Comparing both shows, the biggest difference is size. There are four times as many attendees at the Consumer Electronics Show.

    Fong: Yes, and another difference is these shows clearly represent two separate markets for us, the U.S. and Europe. Both are high priorities, but I think we should focus on the U.S. market first. Once we get our foot in the door there, we can then expand to England and Europe.

    Lee: The main similarity I see between the two shows is that many of the big name electronics firms—Microsoft, Intel, Compaq, IBM—will be exhibiting at both shows. But the Las Vegas show will attract manufacturers, wholesalers, distributors, and retailers from all over North America. We need to get our name out there, and the Consumer Electronics Show is the place to do it.

    Wang: Well I think U.S. distributors and retailers are obviously our major target outside Asia at this point. All right then, why don't we get a booth and do whatever it takes to put on a good show in Las Vegas? Do you both agree with that plan, and are you both available in January?

Fong: Sounds like a solid plan, and I am definitely available in January. I'd like to work on the design of our booth in Las Vegas. It's got to be glitzy.

Lee: Yeah, I like the plan, and I'm available too. Besides that, I'm good at black jack!

Answers: 1. F   2. T   3. F   4. T   5. T

Language Mastery (page 70)

3. a. A Mercedes Benz is far more expensive than a Honda Civic.
    b. Sales for this year are much less than for last year.
    c. Jim is a more effective manager than our previous boss.
    d. They placed fewer orders this year than last year.
    e. Profits for this quarter are about the same as last quarter's.
    f. The company has far fewer employees after the restructuring.
    g. More employees are signing up for retirement plans.
    h. Our budget is similar to last year's.

Answers:

a. much more	c. more	e. the same	g. more
b. much less	d. less	f. much less	h. the same

Unit 14. Making Airline Reservations

Listening Practice (page 73)

A. Agent: United International Desk, this is Sally. How <u>may I help you?</u>

Ms. Fong: Yes, I'd like <u>to check on flights</u> from Singapore to Las Vegas, Nevada.

Agent: When are you <u>planning on traveling?</u>

Ms. Fong: I do have some flexibility, but I need to be in Las Vegas <u>by January 7th at the latest</u> and return on the 12th.

Agent: Let's see. We have a <u>direct flight</u> to Las Vegas with one-hour stops in Tokyo and Los Angeles. You could leave Singapore <u>on Flight 320 at 8:00 A.M.</u> on January 6th, arriving in Las Vegas at 12:36 P.M. the same day.

Ms. Fong: And what about the return?

Agent: You'd leave Las Vegas on <u>Flight 344 at 8:05</u> A.M. on January 12th, arriving in Singapore <u>at 11:45 P.M.</u> the following day.

Ms. Fong: How <u>long is the flight?</u>

Agent: Nineteen hours and thirty-six minutes.

Ms. Fong: Boy, that's a long flight! And how much is it?

Agent: The round-trip ticket is <u>U.S.$1,044.</u>

Ms. Fong: OK, I think I'd like to go ahead and make a reservation.

Agent: All right, Ms. Fong, your reservation number is <u>19140M (as in Mary).</u> I can hold this reservation for 24 hours.

Language Mastery (page 75)

2. Travel Agent: Good morning, Travel Solutions. How may I help you?

Paul Nelson: Yes, this is Paul Nelson with IBM in Los Angeles. I'd like to get a flight to Seattle on February 17th and return on the 21st.

Travel Agent: How many traveling in your party, sir?

Paul Nelson: Just one.

Travel Agent: There are several flights to Seattle. When would you like to leave?

Paul Nelson: Let's see. I'd like to catch an early flight out and return in the evening on the 21st.

Travel Agent: All right. I have a flight leaving L.A. at 6:00 A.M. arriving in Seattle at 9:20. Is that too early?

Paul Nelson:		No, that's fine. And what about the return?
Travel Agent:		I can put you on a 7:00 P.M. flight arriving back in L.A. at 9:30. How does that sound?
Paul Nelson:		Sounds good. And I need a hotel for the four nights in Seattle.
Travel Agent:		Do you have a hotel preference?
Paul Nelson:		I'd like to be downtown. The Sheraton or the Hilton would be nice.
Travel Agent:		Okay, I'll check that for you. Do you have any special requests?
Paul Nelson:		Oh, yes. Since I'll be arriving early in the day, could you request an early check-in? I'd like to drop off my bags before going to a meeting.
Travel Agent:		Certainly.

3.
Mr. Wang:	Could you please tell me how to get to the Hyatt Hotel on Market Street?
Information Clerk:	Sure. You've got several possibilities. You could take a taxi. It takes about 30 minutes and costs about $30.00.
Mr. Wang:	So what else is there?
Information Clerk:	You could catch one of the local shuttle services. The cost is about $22.00. Or you could take the city bus to the bus terminal for about $6.00.
Mr. Wang:	So where do I catch the shuttle?
Information Clerk:	Go out the doors to the middle island. You'll see signs for the different shuttle services. Tell one of the agents where you want to go.
Mr. Wang:	OK, thanks for your help.

4.
Man:	Just arrived in San Francisco today?
Mr. Wang:	Yeah. Everything went smoothly. Not like my last trip to Miami. It was a nightmare!
Man:	Really? What happened?
Mr. Wang:	Oh, you don't want to hear it.
Man:	No, I do. I'm curious now.
Mr. Wang:	Well, first of all, when I got to the airport in Taipei, I realized that I didn't have my passport.
Man:	So what did you do?
Mr. Wang:	I called my wife. She drove like crazy in rush hour traffic to get it to me. I almost missed my flight. And then when I got to Miami, someone brushed up against me at the airport. And then I realized my wallet was gone.
Man:	Oh, no! Someone stole your wallet? What did you do about your credit cards and money?
Mr. Wang:	I had to cancel my credit cards right away, but the cash was gone. Luckily, I always travel with two credit cards—one in my wallet and one in my briefcase.
Man:	Good for you. And was that it, I mean, the end of your problems?
Mr. Wang:	I wish! When I checked into my hotel in Miami, they couldn't find my reservation. And then later that night, I went to get some ice on my floor at the hotel, and I locked myself out. But that's not all. The final straw was when I got a cab in Miami to go back to the airport.
Man:	What happened?
Mr. Wang:	I got in the cab, but one block later, the cab broke down. I couldn't believe it.
Man:	That's incredible! Well, let's hope your stay in San Francisco turns out better!

Unit 15. Booking a Hotel, Checking In, and Checking Out

Listening Practice (page 78)

A.	*Travel Agent:*	If you're interested in Las Vegas, let me give you some information about three convention hotels: Caesar's Palace, the Mirage, and the Triple Crown. The Triple Crown is one block from the convention center, the Mirage is three blocks, and Caesar's Palace is two miles.
	Leslie:	And what are the rates for a single room?
	Travel Agent:	Well, the rates are $275.00 for a single at Caesar's Palace, $229.00 at the Mirage, and $183.00 at the Triple Crown.
	Leslie:	And is there much difference between the amenities at the hotels?
	Travel Agent:	Let me check. The Mirage has a business center, a pool, a health spa and salon, a gym, personal fitness trainers, gourmet restaurants, free parking, gambling, nightly shows, shopping, a tropical rain forest, a giant aquarium—you name it! At Caesar's, they have business services, a swimming pool, an exercise room, gambling, and nightly shows. And at the Triple Crown, they have business services, swimming pools, and gambling.
	Leslie:	What about the size of the hotels?
	Travel Agent:	Let's see. Caesar's Palace has 2,400 rooms, the Mirage has 3,000, and the Triple Crown has 800. By the way, Caesar's Palace offers a complimentary continental breakfast, the Mirage offers a complimentary full breakfast buffet, and the Triple Crown doesn't provide breakfast.
	Leslie:	OK, thanks for your help.

Language Mastery (page 80)

2.	*Front Desk:*	Can I help the next person in line please?
	Leslie Fong:	I'd like to check in. I have a reservation.
	Front Desk:	Your last name, please?
	Leslie Fong:	Fong, F-O-N-G, Leslie.
	Front Desk:	Oh, yes, I have your reservation. You're checking out on the 11th?
	Leslie Fong:	Yes, that's right.
	Front Desk:	OK. We have you staying five nights at the conference rate of $229.00 per night. Would you like smoking or non?
	Leslie Fong:	Nonsmoking.
	Front Desk:	And would you prefer a king-sized bed or two queens?
	Leslie Fong:	A king would be great.
	Front Desk:	Ms. Fong, I'll need to take an imprint of your credit card. (after a few minutes) OK, you'll be in room 2425. Only one key for you, ma'am?
	Leslie Fong:	One key is fine.
	Front Desk:	Would you like a minibar key?
	Leslie Fong:	Sure.
	Front Desk:	OK, Ms. Fong. Here is the key to your room; you'll be in room 2425 on the twenty-fourth floor. Would you like help with your luggage?
	Leslie Fong:	Oh, no, thanks.
5.	*Front Desk:*	Yes?
	Leslie Fong:	I'd like to check out, please.
	Front Desk:	Your room number?
	Leslie Fong:	2425.
	Front Desk:	One moment while I print out your bill.
	Leslie Fong:	(Looks over the bill) Hmm, I thought the rate was $229 per night. What's this charge of $22.90 per night?
	Front Desk:	Oh, that's a 10 percent room tax.
	Leslie Fong:	Oh, OK. And this shows that I have a $17.50 minibar bill. I didn't use the minibar.

Front Desk:	Oh, I'm terribly sorry. This must be a mistake. I'll correct it for you right away. Do you want to put your charges on this card?
Leslie Fong:	Yes. (signs it)
Front Desk:	OK. Here's your copy, Ms. Fong. I hope you enjoyed your stay.

Unit 16. Describing Products at a Trade Show

Listening Practice (page 82)

A.	*Mr. Wang:*	Can <u>I answer any questions?</u>
	Sarah Adams:	Well, yes. I've been to this show several times, and I haven't seen TaiCom before. Is this <u>your first time here?</u>
	Mr. Wang:	Yes, as a matter of fact. We've only been in business for a few years and have been concentrating primarily on Asia up to this point.
	Sarah Adams:	Well, I hope it <u>turns out to be a good show for you.</u> By the way, I'm Sarah Adams, purchasing manager for Computer City. So tell me about your computers.
	Mr. Wang:	Hi Sarah. I'm Li-ting Wang. Well, you can find anything you want at this show, but where we really excel is in <u>offering high performance</u> at a great price.
	Sarah Adams:	We're always <u>looking for good value.</u> How do your prices compare with Compaq's, for example?
	Mr. Wang:	<u>We're very competitive,</u> and with the exchange rates what they are right now, we're a terrific value.
	Sarah Adams:	Well, that sounds interesting. Listen, I don't have much time right now—but I'd be <u>very interested in talking with you</u> in more detail when I get home.
	Mr. Wang:	Great. Here, <u>let me give you my card,</u> a price list, and some literature about our products to take with you.
	Sarah Adams:	Oh, thanks. And here's my card.
	Mr. Wang:	<u>Thanks for stopping by,</u> and I'll give you a call when I get back.

Module 5

Unit 17. A Business Lunch

Listening Practice (page 88)

Rick:	Rick Masterson.
Edmundo:	Hello, Rick. This is Edmundo Orsi. We met a few weeks ago at the Ministry of Trade reception in Buenos Aires.
Rick:	Yes, of course. Nice to hear from you, Edmundo!
Edmundo:	I'm in town this week, so I thought I'd call to see what you're up to.
Rick:	Well, I've been keeping busy. We've been interviewing for a couple of new positions here.
Edmundo:	Yes, finding the right people really takes time. Well, how about lunch one day this week?
Rick:	That would be great. When is good for you?
Edmundo:	Let's see—I guess any day except Friday. When are you free?
Rick:	What about Wednesday?
Edmundo:	Sure. Uh, what do you recommend in the area? Is there a good place close to you?
Rick:	We could go to Julia's on Pennsylvania Avenue. Terrific food. What do you think?
Edmundo:	Sounds great. Could you give me directions?
Rick:	Why don't you meet me at my office, and we'll walk over together? I'm at 1700 West Fifteenth Avenue, on the sixth floor.

Edmundo:	Good. 1700 West Fifteenth Avenue, sixth floor. OK, well, shall I come by about noon?
Rick:	Noon's good. I'll look for you.
Edmundo:	OK. See you Wednesday.
Rick:	You bet. See you then. Bye.

Listening Practice (page 89)

1. Hi, this is Lisa. I wanted to let you know that I'm having a few people over on Friday after work. Can you join us—about 5:00? I'll have some munchies and some brews. I'm inviting all of our work group and a few other people. Hope to see you.

2. Hello. This is Dave Smith. I wanted to invite you to a reception at SM Industries to celebrate the launch of our new line of motion detectors. It's going to be next Friday afternoon at 4:00. There'll be an open bar and a buffet dinner served about 5:30. You'll be getting an invitation in the mail, but I thought I'd give you a little advance notice. Please join us. Bye.

3. Hi, this is Sylvia Hollings. I'm hoping you can join us for a small dinner party at my house on the 17th, at about 7:00. Several other people from our department will be there. Could you let me know if you can come? You can just RSVP at work when you see me. Talk to you soon.

munchies: snack food
brews: beers
motion detector: device that "sees" motion
RSVP: respond yes or no to an invitation

Unit 18. Ordering Food

Listening Practice (page 93)

1. I'd like to start with the mushrooms with chèvre.
2. I'll take the salmon fillet, please.
3. I'd like the fettuccine and roast duck.
4. We'll start out with Cajun spiced calamari.
5. Uh, I'd like the filet mignon.
6. Let's see. I think I'll start with the lobster-shrimp ravioli.
7. I'd like to try the shrimp Nancy.
8. Could we start with the eggplant ravioli?

Unit 19. Ordering Drinks

Listening Practice (page 99)

Waitperson:	What can I bring you?
First Woman:	Well, let's see. . . . I'd like a glass of white wine.
Waitperson:	All right. And for you, ma'am?
Second Woman:	And I'd like a scotch on the rocks with a splash of water.
First Man:	What do you have on draft?
Waitperson:	Bud, Bud Light, Coors, Coors Light, and Foster's Pale Ale.
First Man:	Do you have any imported beers?
Waitperson:	Yes, besides Foster's we've got Dos Equis, San Miguel, Moosehead, and Sapporo.
First Man:	Uh, I think I'll just have a Bud.
Waitperson:	And for you, sir?
Second Man:	Oh, sorry, I wasn't paying attention. What kind of beer do you have?
First Man:	Whew! Just get a Bud.
Second Man:	Do you have Guinness?

Waitperson:	I'm afraid not.
Second Man:	OK. A Bud for me, too.
Waitperson:	Very good. I'll be right back with your drinks.

scotch on the rocks with a splash of water: with ice and a little water

Unit 20. Etiquette in Social Situations

Listening Practice (page 102)

A. *Edmundo:* You know, I went to a seminar on cross-cultural behavior recently. Is it true what they say about personal space? You know, I think South Americans stand closer together than people in the United States when they talk.

Rick: Yeah. The customs are different. We usually stand several feet apart. In fact, we're uncomfortable standing closer.

Edmundo: I guess there're probably a lot of differences in business, too.

Rick: Some. It's funny. Whether a certain behavior is polite or a faux pas depends on what country you're in.

Edmundo: Right. I'm keeping an eye open to differences while I'm here. You know what they say, "When in Rome, do as the Romans do!"

Rick: Good point. I usually try to find out something about the customs in countries I visit, too.

Edmundo: Yeah, it's getting easier these days. People are becoming more aware of cultural differences.

Rick: And it's equally true that anyone making an honest attempt to adapt to local customs will be well received just about anywhere in the world.

Edmundo: I think so, too.

etiquette: polite behavior in social situations
faux pas: a social mistake /fo pa/

Listening Practice (page 103)

A. 1. – Did you hear him? He made all this noise when he ate, and he slurped his soup. He was burping and belching loudly after the meal. Sounded like a piece of heavy machinery.

2. – I don't understand why Jennifer didn't tip the waitress. I was so embarrassed.

3. – He was just going on and on. I mean, everybody likes to talk during a meal, but I was taught to take small bites so it's possible to talk without upsetting your dinner companions.

4. + Oh, she was the perfect hostess! She introduced everyone so nicely and remembered everyone's name.

5. + Did you see how he stood up when Ms. Sheffield came in? I was so impressed with his manners.

6. – Did you see how much he was drinking? I counted three. A beer to relax or something, but during a business meal, I just can't imagine drinking that much.

7. – I enjoyed the meal but not people's manners. People were reaching to get things at the table instead of asking for them to be passed. Where are people's manners these days?

Language Mastery (page 105)

2. a. correspondence
   b. luggage or baggage
   c. equipment
   d. beef

  e. information
  f. wines
  g. cash or money

Module 6

Unit 21. Starting a Discussion

Listening Practice (page 109)

A. *Michael:*   Julie, <u>have you got a moment?</u> I wanted to talk with you about Spyder.
 Julie: Sure. Let's go into my office. <u>What's on your mind?</u>
 Michael: Well, Spyder's been making inroads with Japanese retailers—especially the high-end stores—ever since they started sponsoring Olympic ski racers. <u>I wonder if we need</u> to think seriously about carrying some of their lines.
 Julie: Well, yeah. They seem eager to work with us. When's the rep coming?
 Michael: Friday. Thomas Grant.
 Julie: That's right. OK. You know, <u>one thing I'm a little worried about is</u> the reaction of our Japanese manufacturers to more competing lines.
 Michael: Everyone's got to compete in the global economy, don't you think? It's not as though anyone has exclusive rights with us. If we can get high quality at good prices, we need to go with it. <u>By the way,</u> Thomas Grant's been by once before. Remember him?

Language Mastery (page 112)

2. a. Have you got a minute? I wanted to make a suggestion. I really think we need to consider having <u>more frequent meetings.</u> Once a month isn't enough.
 b. I've been thinking about how we handle customer complaints. I think we need to <u>follow up with an e-mail.</u> That way we could make sure that we're responding quickly.
 c. Could we talk for a moment? You know, I wonder if we should <u>start visiting our big clients more frequently.</u> Most of our competitors do. I'm not really sure everyone agrees with me.
 d. S'cuse me. Do you have a moment? I wondered what <u>your reaction</u> was <u>to that proposal</u> yesterday. Oh, sorry. You seem busy right now. Maybe I should come back later.
 e. Hey, what's happening in your department? <u>I need to hear from you guys more frequently.</u> I haven't seen anyone from HR for some time. What's going on?
 f. Just wondered if you'd decided <u>how to handle Smith. Is he fired?</u>

Unit 22. Giving Opinions, Agreeing, and Disagreeing

Listening Practice (page 115)

A. *Michael:*   So, Julie, <u>do you think we'll have</u> enough demand for this high-end skiwear?
 Julie: These lines really <u>caught on during the Winter Olympics.</u> Remember? People were asking for Spyder, but it was only available in Tokyo. I think <u>they'll do well.</u>
 Michael: <u>I sure hope you're right.</u> I think we should order in quantity and see if we can get a discount.
 Julie: <u>I'm not so sure about that.</u> Let's think about this a little more. You know, <u>it might be better to</u> try a smaller order and see what happens.
 Michael: Really? Well, I suppose so. That's not as risky.

Language Mastery (page 116)

1. A. 1. As far as our department is concerned—the order is too large. (opinion)
      2. This is a large order—over 50 different parts. (fact)
      3. It's 10:52 A.M. (fact)
      4. I think investing in stocks is the best way to make money. (opinion)
      5. In my view, the company should file for bankruptcy. (opinion)
      6. The company never had a bad credit rating in over 20 years. (fact)
      7. At 5:00, most of my co-workers are still at their desks. (fact)
      8. My colleague left the office a few minutes ago. (fact)

   B. 1. I suppose so. <u>agreement</u> ☑ mild
      2. Really? I don't think so. <u>disagreement</u> ☑ medium
      3. You're absolutely right. I think we should put the new policy into effect right now. <u>agreement</u> ☑ strong
      4. I'm not so sure that's a good idea. Maybe you should hold off on the advertising campaign. <u>diagreement</u> ☑ mild
      5. You bet. That's exactly right. <u>agreement</u> ☑ strong
      6. I couldn't agree more; staff should always be improving their skills. <u>agreement</u> ☑ strong

Unit 23. Developing the Discussion

Listening Practice (page 119)

A. **Thomas:** It's great to see you again. How's business these days?

Julie: <u>Good to see you too,</u> Thomas. Business is pretty good. The Japanese economy is doing well, so we're optimistic about this quarter. Last quarter wasn't our best.

Thomas: Hey, maybe what you need is some exciting new skiwear lines. You know, Japanese consumers see Spyder at every Winter Olympics. This stuff is hot! <u>I also think they'd sell well</u> in Japan because Japanese consumers want high quality, and these lines are exceptional.

Julie: Well, frankly, <u>we'd like to try them.</u> I'm a little hesitant, though. Spyder is largely untested in Japan. <u>Another reason I hesitate is that</u> they're expensive, and I don't want to have to discount my prices to retailers too much.

Thomas: OK. Well, there isn't really much risk to you as a distributor. We can handle your first purchase on a sale or return basis. If they don't sell, you can return them. Also, your customers can always return the item to the company for a refund. We've got a lifetime guarantee. <u>And that's another good reason to</u> carry Spyder products. We want to make everything as easy as possible for you.

Unit 24. Summarizing Views and Making Suggestions

Listening Practice (page 124)

A. **Michael:** So how did the meeting go?

Julie: I had a good discussion with Thomas.

Michael: Yeah? What did he have to say?

Julie: Well, for one thing, he told me that we could place our first order sale or return. Pretty nice—no risk to us.

Michael: That's great. So you feel confident about placing an order?

Julie: I really do. Thomas answered all my questions, and I feel great about Spyder products. He told me something about their lifetime guarantee too, but I can't remember who customers return the product to—the retailer or the company. We should also ask him for some brochures for our retailers.

Michael:	So you want me to ask him about the lifetime guarantee and about getting some brochures when I place an order?
Julie:	That would be great, Michael. Uh, let's get about 100 of both styles.
Michael:	OK, I'll get our usual numbers of small, medium, large, and extra large. Uh, that's Picabo and Quest, right?
Julie:	Yeah. We liked those two styles best. And why don't you see if we can get them delivered to the warehouse before my trip to Japan next month?

Language Mastery (page 126)

2. a. I don't want to sound overly negative, but I'm just not sure about that proposal your team made. You need a solution that interfaces better with technology. Why don't the three of you talk to Dave to get some input?

b. I'm not really sure why, but I'd prefer we waited a few weeks to launch our online business. I don't feel that we are ready to go online yet. We need more time to take care of glitches in our ordering process.

c. I'm not sure exactly where we stand on this. Are we going to invest in R&D or not? I think we need to set a clear policy. We can't go halfway on this. It's all or nothing.

d. I don't understand why we don't have agreement on this issue. It seems clear that our efforts to recycle will improve our corporate image.

Information Files

File 1

[Instructor: Enlarge this material when photocopying, if possible.]

How do you do?
Hi. I'm (name).
Everything's going well.
Will you excuse me?
Fine, thanks.
Please call me (first name).
Yes, I've only been here two days.
Sure. See you later.
How do you do?
Sure. If you'll call me (first name).
How's it going?
My name's (name).
Hi. You're new here, aren't you?
How are you?

File 2

As the human resources manager for your company, you need to do several things.

- When asked, tell the CEO your agenda item: human resources requirements for the product launch. Indicate that you would like this topic to be at the end of the agenda.
- Listen carefully as the other managers discuss their requirements. Since all of your departments consist of only a few people, make note of how many additional people may be needed in different areas as the managers discuss their plans. You might even want to ask them, "How many additional people or working hours per week will that require in your department?" After you get a total, try to estimate the total costs involved for the extra personnel.

- React to others' ideas as often as possible, especially when it might mean additional personnel or have other effects on HR or training issues.
- Help members be constructive in their comments. Put a positive spin on things.
- Help the CEO summarize views and mention areas of agreement toward the end of the meeting.

Be sure to ask for other people's ideas about your human resources plans too.

File 3

Take a few minutes to review the information about General Electric and then be ready to answer your partner's questions.

General Electric Company

- Formed in 1892 by consolidating Edison General Electric Company and Thomas-Houston Company
- 12 divisions: aircraft engines, appliances, capital services, lighting, medical systems, NBC, plastics, power systems, electrical distribution and controls
- Employees: 239,000
- Headquarters: Fairfield, Connecticut, USA
- Annual sales last year: $90.81 billion

Now ask your colleague these questions about Procter & Gamble:

What do you know about the history of the company?
When was the company founded?
What does the company produce?
How many people does the company employ?
Where is the company located?
What were the company's annual sales last year?

File 4

As the advertising manager for your company, please prepare in these areas.

- When asked, tell the CEO your agenda item: advertising during the product launch.
- Think about how and where you want to advertise. Will you need to have TV advertising, or will advertising in magazines or newspapers be best? Suggest an advertising plan for the product launch including where you will advertise and how often. Come up with an estimate of your total costs.
- Be sure to ask for other people's ideas about your advertising plans. Ask for suggestions and react to any ideas that might work especially well.
- During the entire discussion, react when others contribute ideas, especially if these ideas concern your area.

File 5

Take the role of Richard Carmichael.

Nicole: Well, it's really been good to have a chance to talk with you in more detail. Unfortunately, I need to get back to the office for a 2:00 appointment.

Richard: _____ . Let's see. I'll walk back with you—I'm going to tour the production facility. _____ seeing exactly what these trains look like.

[Back at TVE headquarters]

Nicole: It's been a pleasure, Richard. I'll introduce you to Robert Cartier, and he'll take you over to the production facility and show you around.

Richard: You've been so helpful. I appreciate all the information you've given me. I'm _____ the tour.

Nicole:	Yes. I hope you enjoy it. . . . Ah, Richard, let me introduce Robert Cartier, our public relations manager. Robert, this is Richard Carmichael from the California Department of Transportation.
Richard:	_____ , Mr. Cartier? _____ meet you.
Robert:	How do you do, Mr. Carmichael? My pleasure.
Nicole:	Richard's ready to see the production facility now. I'll see you both tomorrow. Will you excuse me?
Richard:	Sure. _____ tomorrow, Nicole. And thanks for lunch.

File 6

As the finance manager for your company, please prepare in these areas.

- When asked, tell the CEO your agenda item: the budget for the product launch.
- Think about the product or service your group is offering. Decide on a reasonable budget amount for marketing and advertising during the product launch. (How long a time is involved for the launch?) Try to find a balance between limiting costs and spending too much.
- Listen very carefully when the marketing manager talks about plans so that you can adjust your amount if necessary. React to any item of discussion that involves cost.
- During the entire discussion, react to any ideas that might put the company at financial risk; you're the one who needs to be sure of monetary responsibility.

Be sure to ask for other people's ideas about your plans too.

File 7

Tell your colleague about the prices for women's skiwear. Begin with, "OK, now I'd like to tell you a little about pricing for high-end skiwear for women." Then give each brand name below and the prices; for example, Spyder Picabo is $599.

High-End Skiwear Pricing by Brand

Women's Skiwear

Spyder Picabo	$599
Nuages	$529
Xpressions	$449
Blue Skies	$429

File 8

Ask your partner these questions about General Electric Corporation. Before you begin, look briefly at the information below about P&G so that you can answer questions also.

What do you know about the history of General Electric?
When was the company founded?
What does the company produce?
How many people does the company employ?
Where is the company located?
What were the company's annual sales last year?

Review this information about Procter & Gamble and be ready to answer your partner's questions.

Procter & Gamble

- The company was founded in 1837 by William Procter and James Gamble. They started making and selling soap and candles.
- The company produces a wide range of consumer products including soaps, laundry detergent, shampoos, cosmetics, toothpaste, diapers, paper products.
- The company employs about 103,000 people worldwide.
- Headquarters: Cincinnati, Ohio, USA
- Annual sales for last year: $36.7 billion

File 9

Take the roles of Nicole Legrand and Richard Carmichael.

Nicole: Well, it's _____ to have a chance to talk with you in more detail. Unfortunately, I need to get back to the office for a 2:00 appointment.

Richard: No problem. Let's see. I'll walk back with you—I'm going to tour the production facility. I'm interested in seeing exactly what these trains look like.

[Back at TVE headquarters]

Nicole: _____ , Richard. I'll introduce you to Robert Cartier, and he will take you over to the production facility and show you around.

Richard: You've been so helpful. I appreciate all the information you've given me. I'm looking forward to the tour.

Nicole: Yes. I hope you enjoy it. . . . Ah, Richard, _____ _____ introduce Robert Cartier, our public relations manager. Robert, _____ Richard Carmichael from the California Department of Transportation.

Richard: How do you do, Mr. Cartier? Pleased to meet you.

Robert: _____ , Mr. Carmichael? My _____ .

Nicole: Richard's ready to see the production facility now. _____ _____ . Will you excuse me?

Richard: Sure. _____ , Nicole. And thanks for lunch.

File 10

You will take the role of Sung-Wook Jung. While you are in San Francisco next week, you would like to have a lunch meeting with Terry Smith, who is the procurement manager at Cellular Technology, Inc. They have purchased electronic parts from you in the past. Call Terry and tell her you will be in town next week. Try to set up a lunch meeting.

Sung-Wook Jung's Calendar

Time	Monday	Tuesday	Wednesday	Thursday	Friday
9:00		Tour of SRG subsidiary mfg. plant		Meeting with Fred Stone of Sun, Inc.	Golf with Fred Hanks
10:00	Arrive in San Francisco				
11:00					
12:00	Check in at the Marriott Hotel				
1:00	Lunch			Lunch with R. J. Watts	
2:00			Meeting with Jack Lee at Global Telecom		
3:00					Check out of hotel
4:00					
5:00	Dinner meeting with SRG rep.			Giants baseball game	Leave for Seoul

File 11

As the marketing manager for your company, please prepare in these areas.

- When asked, tell the CEO your agenda item: the marketing plan.
- To be able to tell the group about your marketing plans, answer these questions. Your answers will help the group make decisions about what kind of marketing plan is good for your product or service: What is going to be the best way to sell

the product or service? What kind of person is your target market? What kinds of stores or other outlets will you use? How will you convince people to buy? What other specific marketing ideas do you have for this product launch?

- What support do you need from advertising, human resources, or other departments?
- What else do you need from your company to ensure a successful product launch?
- During the entire discussion, react to any ideas that might affect the success of your marketing effort.

Be sure to ask for other people's ideas about your marketing plan too.

File 12

You are Leslie Fong of TaiCom, and you are calling to make a reservation for yourself and two of your colleagues at the Mirage Hotel in Las Vegas.

You want three rooms for January 7th–12th. Before you make your reservation, you want to know the following:

the rate per night for a single, a double, and a suite
- availability
- if the price includes breakfast
- if the hotel has a business center for your use and what computer equipment is available
- if the rooms are wired for Internet access
- what other amenities are available at the hotel

If you like what the hotel offers, book two single rooms and one suite.

File 13

You will play the part of Terry Smith, procurement manager at Cellular Technology, Inc. You are in charge of purchasing all parts and equipment for your company. You have bought parts from SRG Electronics before and have been very pleased with the quality and price. When Sung-Wook Jung calls to arrange a time to meet, look at your calendar and see what you can arrange.

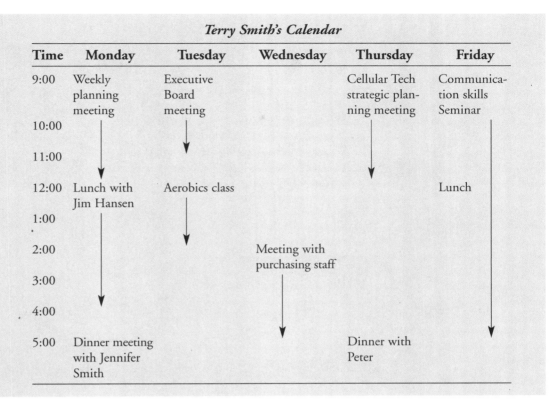

Terry Smith's Calendar

Time	Monday	Tuesday	Wednesday	Thursday	Friday
9:00	Weekly planning meeting	Executive Board meeting		Cellular Tech strategic planning meeting	Communication skills Seminar
10:00					
11:00					
12:00	Lunch with Jim Hansen	Aerobics class			Lunch
1:00					
2:00			Meeting with purchasing staff		
3:00					
4:00					
5:00	Dinner meeting with Jennifer Smith			Dinner with Peter	

File 14

As the CEO for your company, you need to do several things:

- Begin the meeting by asking for agenda items to include in the discussion. Write down the agenda items to use during the meeting.
- Run the meeting, going through all of your agenda items. Try to include everyone and call on group members to discuss their plans and what they need to succeed. If these items are not already on the agenda, be sure to ask about the marketing plan, the budget for the launch, the advertising program, and HR considerations.
- React to any ideas that might work especially well or put the company at risk.
- Summarize views after each speaker and mention areas of agreement as they come up.
- Conclude the meeting.

While other members are planning what they will say, consider your role carefully. You will need to listen very carefully and help with communication. It's your job to restate people's views so that there is no misunderstanding. When members seem ready, begin the meeting by asking for agenda items.

File 15

1. What are you doing for lunch tomorrow?
2. What about some golf this weekend?
3. What about having dinner tonight?
4. You want to play tennis this weekend?
5. You want to go for a drink after work?

File 16

You are the front desk clerk at the Mirage Hotel in Las Vegas.

Answer the phone by giving the name of the hotel and ask how you may help.

For the dates requested, tell the caller that most of your rooms are booked because of the Consumer Electronics Show. However, tell the caller you do have one double room at $250.00 per night, one single at $229.00 per night, and a suite that sleeps two and is suitable for entertaining at $500 per night.

The double room has two queen-sized beds, the single has one king-sized bed, and the suite has a queen-sized bed and a sofa that converts into a queen-sized bed.

All rooms have king or queen beds, air conditioning, a minibar, a coffee maker, Internet access, and a complimentary buffet breakfast in the garden restaurant.

Amenities include a fully equipped business center with IBM and Mac computers, a scanner, a fax machine, a photocopy machine, a swimming pool, a fitness room, nightly entertainment, a tropical rain forest, a giant aquarium, and gambling.

Make sure to get the caller's name, daytime phone number, and credit card number to reserve the room.

File 17

1. Are you free for lunch in the next week or so?
2. What about a game of racquet ball this week?
3. You want to get some dinner?
4. Let's get a drink after work. Want to?
5. How about going to that Internet seminar next week?

File 18

Take the part of Michael. Be ready to help your partner with Julie's part. Anything that is appropriate is OK. After you practice, change roles.

Michael: So how did the meeting go?

Julie: I had a good discussion with Thomas.

Michael: Yeah? What did he _____ ?

Julie: Well, for one thing, he told me that we could place our first order sale or return. Pretty nice—no risk to us.

Michael: That's great. _____

confident about placing an order?

Julie: I really do. Thomas answered all my questions, and I feel great about Spyder products. He told me something about their lifetime guarantee too, but I can't remember who customers return the product to, the retailer or the company. We should also ask him for some brochures for our retailers.

Michael: _____ me to ask him about the lifetime guarantee and about getting some brochures when I place an order?

Julie: That would be great, Michael. Uh, let's get about 100 of both styles.

Michael: OK, I'll get our usual numbers of small, medium, large, and extra large. Uh, that's Picabo and Quest, _____ _____ ?

Julie: Yeah. We liked those two styles best. And why don't you see if we can get them delivered to the warehouse before my trip to Japan next month?

File 19

1. saucepan and frying pan
2. soy sauce, ketchup (catsup), mustard
3. coffeepot, cream and sugar
4. teapot
5. butter and butter knife
6. six-pack of soda
7. coffee mug
8. salt and pepper
9. pitcher of water
10. oil and vinegar (for a salad)
11. basket of bread
12. wine in an ice bucket
13. bottle opener and corkscrew
14. place setting with dinner plate, bread plate, water glass, wineglass, coffee cup and saucer, napkin, salad fork, dinner fork, knife, spoon, and dessert spoon above the plate

File 20

Computer City's Purchasing Manager

You have been selling Compaq, IBM, HP, Apple, and Packard Bell computers for the past year, and they have been very popular. You learned about TaiCom's new

4800 computer at the Las Vegas Trade Show. You are calling TaiCom's marketing manager to find out more information about this new computer. Specifically, you want to know the following:

Performance: Memory:
Other features:
Customer support:
Wholesale price: Warranty period:
When it will be available:
Minimum order: Delivery time:
Terms:

File 21

Take the part of Julie. Be ready to help your partner with Michael's part. Anything that is appropriate is OK. After you practice, change roles.

Michael: So how did the meeting go?

Julie: I had _____ with

Thomas.

Michael: Yeah? What did he have to say?

Julie: Well, _____ , he told me

that we could place our first order sale or return. Pretty nice—no risk

to us.

Michael: That's great. So you feel confident about placing an order?

Julie: I really do. Thomas answered _____

_____ , and I feel great about Spyder products. He told me

something _____ , but I

can't remember who customers return the product to, the retailer or

the company. We _____

for some brochures for our retailers.

Michael: So you want me to ask him about the lifetime guarantee and about

getting some brochures when I place an order?

Julie: That would be great, Michael. Uh, _____

_____ about 100 of both styles.

Michael: OK, I'll get our usual numbers of small, medium, large, and extra large. Uh, that's Picabo and Quest, right?

Julie: Yeah. We liked those two styles best. And _____ _____ if we can get them delivered to the warehouse before my trip to Japan next month?

File 22

Edmundo: What would you like _____ ?

Rick: I think I'll just have some iced tea.

Edmundo: Excuse me. What do you _____ ?

Waitperson: Bud, Bud Light, Miller, Miller Light, Moosehead, and Guinness Stout.

Edmundo: OK. Let's see. Iced tea _____ , and I'll have a Moosehead.

Waitperson: All right. I'll be right back with your drinks.

Rick: Uh, you know, a Moosehead sounds great. I'd like to change my order.

Waitperson: So, two Mooseheads?

Rick: Yeah. Thanks.

Waitperson: You bet. Back in a moment to take your food order.

File 23

Listen to what your partner reads to you. Repeat what he or she says and add one of these endings to complete the sentence.

. . . the next train leaves?
. . . going to rain tomorrow.

. . . my work is good quality.
. . . that costs?

Now read to your partner. Make sure your partner repeats what you say before adding an ending.

Could you tell me how much . . .
Do you know what time . . .
I'd like to know if the boss thinks . . .
I wonder if you know whether it is . . .

File 24

1. This is a popular beer.
   It's very light but has good taste.
   It's made in Colorado. (Answer: Coors)
2. This is a kind of wine.
   It's a type of white wine.
   It's a sparkling wine used for celebrations. (Answer: champagne)
3. This is a popular cocktail.
   It's made with vodka.
   It also has orange juice in it. (Answer: screwdriver)
4. This is a great kind of beer.
   It doesn't come from the US.
   It's a little darker and more full bodied than most U.S. beers.
   It's from Mexico, and its name means "Two Xs." (Answer: Dos Equis)

File 25

Edmundo: What would you like to drink?

Rick: I think I'll just have some iced tea.

Edmundo: Excuse me. What do you have on tap?

Waitperson: _____.

Edmundo: OK. Let's see. Iced tea for my friend, and I'll have a Moosehead.

Waitperson:	All right. I'll be right back with _____ .
Rick:	Uh, you know, a Moosehead sounds great. I'd like to change my order.
Waitperson:	So, _____ ?
Rick:	Yeah. Thanks.
Waitperson:	_____ . Back in a moment to _____ .

File 26

Read these to your partner. Make sure your partner repeats what you say and adds an ending.

Could you tell me how much . . .
Do you know what time . . .
I'd like to know if the boss thinks . . .
I wonder if you know whether it is . . .

Now listen to your partner's sentence beginnings. Repeat what your partner says and complete each sentence with one of these endings.

. . . going to be clear tomorrow.
. . . our report gives all the information.
. . . the training session begins?
. . . the training session will cost?

File 27

Edmundo:	What would you like to drink?
Rick:	I think _____ some iced tea.

Edmundo:	Excuse me. What do you have on tap?
Waitperson:	Bud, Bud Light, Miller, Miller Light, Moosehead, and Guinness Stout.
Edmundo:	OK. Let's see. Iced tea for my friend, and I'll have a Moosehead.
Waitperson:	All right. I'll be right back with your drinks.
Rick:	Uh, you know, a Moosehead sounds great. _____ _____ my order.
Waitperson:	So, two Mooseheads?
Rick:	_____ .
Waitperson:	You bet. Back in a moment to take your food order.

File 28

You will take on three different roles in conversations with a partner: boss, company director, and colleague. Make sure of your role in each conversation. Your partner will speak first. Answer your partner using these guidelines.

Give your partner time to talk.
Comment on the topic.
Disagree, make up a problem or objection.
Say, "Well, OK, I'll think about it," or give another reaction.

After your partner finishes, it will be your turn to begin three conversations. Take the role of someone employed by a manufacturing company, and use the three topics below. Follow these guidelines.

Ask for time to talk.
Introduce your topic.
State your main point.
Justify your main point.

1. You're talking to a supplier. You want the supplier to take back an order of faulty parts.
2. You're talking to your boss. You want the boss to stay late today and meet an important customer.
3. You're talking to a client. You'd like the carmaker to increase the order for car audio systems.

File 29

Read these clues to your partner.

Across

3 A mixed drink made with tequila, triple sec, and lime juice. Served in a salt rimmed glass.
5 The container for beer that is brought to your table when people want to order more than just a glass of beer each
6 The generic name for drinks like Pepsi, Coke, and Sprite
14 A spice that is used as the flavoring in a soft drink: _____ ale
15 Popular drink all over the world. Made from plant leaves and served hot or iced.
16 A type of hard liquor that is often mixed with tonic water for a summertime drink
17 A type of beer that has a lot of reddish color (two words)
18 A summertime nonalcoholic drink made from lemon juice and water
19 A popular beer from Mexico. The name means "two Xs" (two words)

File 30

[Instructor: Include the numbers when photocopying these sentences to be able to pass out in order. Enlarge this material if possible and cut into strips to pass out to participants.]

1. How much time do you spend online?
2. Studies show that Internet surfers often spend several hours per day on the Internet.
3. Not everyone agrees that this is time well spent.
4. Do you think an hour or two daily is too much?
5. In business, bosses worry if employees spend this kind of time online daily.
6. And what about e-mail?
7. What do you think about employees spending an hour a day reading and answering e-mail?
8. I'm not so sure that we gain efficiency.
9. I think businesses should insist that employees do recreational surfing after hours.

File 31

Read these clues to your partner.

Down
2 Popular hard liquor that is aged for ten years before drinking. Often ordered "on the rocks."
3 The second largest selling U.S. beer
4 A light pink wine
6 A popular lemon lime soda
7 A sparkling "celebration" wine for weddings, New Year's Eve, and special occasions
8 A flavorful, dry red wine
9 A very dry red wine popular with Italian food
10 The U.S. beer with the largest domestic market share
12 A type of beer
13 A popular type of white wine

File 32

Tell your colleague about the prices for men's skiwear. Begin with "Let me tell you a little about pricing for high-end skiwear for men." Then give each brand name below and the prices; for example, Spyder Quest is $859.

High-End Skiwear Pricing by Brand

Men's Skiwear
Spyder Quest $859
Expedition $779
Xpressions $699
Hot Dogger $589

File 33

Did You Spot These Social Mistakes?

- not looking at one's conversational partner
- smoking
- drinking too much
- holding drink in right hand (so that hand is cold and wet when shaking hands)
- talking at the same time as someone else
- taking off jacket
- being dressed too casually for business
- not including someone in the conversational circle

File 34

Have three short discussions with a partner. In each case, you will play the role of someone employed by a manufacturing company. Before you start, think about what you want to say. Follow these guidelines for each of the topics below.

Ask for time to talk.
Introduce your topic.
State your main point.
Justify your main point.

1. You're talking to your boss. You want a promotion now that the manager has been transferred.
2. You're talking to your company director. You want to hire a tech consultant.
3. You're talking to your colleague. You want him or her to work with you on a brochure.

After you have completed these conversations, it will be your partner's turn to begin three conversations. You will play the following roles: supplier, boss, client. Answer your partner using these guidelines.

Give your partner time to talk.
Comment on the topic.
Disagree, make up a problem or an objection.
Say, "Well, OK, I'll think about it," or give another reaction.

File 35

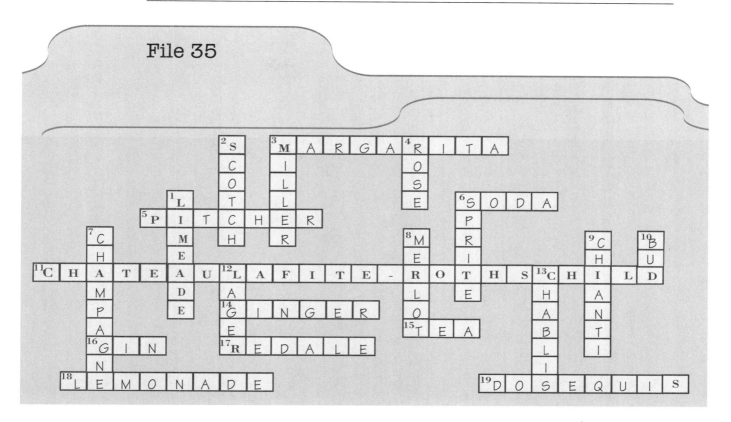

File 36

TaiCom's Marketing Manager

The purchasing manager of Computer City is calling to get more information about your new product the TaiCom 4800 multimedia desktop computer. You hope to establish a good relationship with a potentially large customer. You can provide the following information if asked.

Performance: Intel Pentium III processor with MMX technology; 450 megahertz; 40.0 GB hard drive

Features: DVD-ROM drive, 56K modem, 100 MB Omega Zip drive, high quality video, 3D sound that enables one to take advantage of today's advanced multimedia applications

Excellent customer support, an 800 number, and 24-hour technical support

Wholesale price: U.S.$1,000.00

Delivery time: 15 days from time of order

Warranty: 1 year

Minimum order: 25

It will be available in September.

Terms: Net 30 days

File 37

Answers to the Business Etiquette Quiz

True or False

1. F	6. F	11. T	16. T
2. T	7. F	12. F	17. F
3. F	8. F	13. T	18. F
4. T	9. T	14. T	19. F
5. T	10. F	15. F	20. F

Multiple Choice

1. b, c, d, e	7. b
2. c, d	8. c
3. c	9. a
4. c	10. a
5. d	11. a
6. b	12. c

Language Notes

Tag Questions

Tag questions consist of a statement + a question tag. Only the auxiliary verb *(is, are, was, were, do, did, have, has, had)* is used in the tag.	
The project is coming along well, isn't it?	The first part has statement word order: Subject + Verb. The tag has question word order.
You don't have enough time, do you?	When the statement has a negative (−) verb, the verb in the tag is positive (+).
You have enough time, don't you?	When the statement is positive, the tag is negative.

Tag questions are used to check that information is accurate and to be conversational.

It's beautiful today, isn't it? (conversational)
You got a big increase in salary, didn't you? (check for accuracy)
Our department performed well, didn't it? (conversational)
Their numbers don't agree with ours, do they? (check for accuracy)

Tag questions are used when the speaker thinks it is easy for the listener to agree.

It's beautiful today, isn't it? = I think it's beautiful weather. I'm sure you agree, right?
We haven't had good luck, have we? = Our luck has been bad. Of course you agree, right?

With tag questions, the speaker believes something to be true. The speaker believes the first part (the statement part) is true: "It's beautiful today" and "We haven't had good luck." The speaker expects the listener to agree with this belief. The expected answer agrees with the statement part.

It's beautiful today, isn't it? Expected answer: Yes, it is. Unexpected answer: No, it isn't. (= It's bad weather.)	If the statement part is positive, the expected answer is positive. A negative answer means "I don't agree."
We haven't had good luck, have we? Expected answer: No, we haven't. Unexpected answer: Yes, we have. (= Our luck's OK.)	If the statement part is negative, the expected answer is also negative. A positive answer shows disagreement.

Pronouncing tag questions is tricky. Many questions in English have rising intonation (= the voice goes up at the end). With tag questions, the voice can go up, but it usually goes down. Because the voice goes down so often, tag questions are difficult to understand as questions; they can sound like statements. Compare the pronunciations of these questions.

1. His suggestion doesn't make good sense, does it?   (voice goes down)

2. His suggestion doesn't make good sense, does it?   (voice goes up)

When the speaker's voice goes down as in 1, the meaning is "I am sure of this statement. Please confirm my information." When the speaker's voice goes up as in 2, the meaning is "I am really not entirely sure of this statement; am I correct or not?"

It is a good idea to practice tag questions with the voice falling. If the voice rises all the time on tag questions, the speaker sounds tentative and unsure, not a good quality when doing business with people in the United States. Another good reason to practice with the voice falling is that standardized tests like the TOEIC have a lot of tag questions, usually with falling intonation. If the test taker doesn't understand the tag as a question, he or she will answer incorrectly.

Facts, Figures and Measurements

Numbers

	Cardinal		**Ordinal**
1	one	1st	first
2	two	2nd	second
3	three	3rd	third
4	four	4th	fourth
5	five	5th	fifth
6	six	6th	sixth
7	seven	7th	seventh
8	eight	8th	eighth
9	nine	9th	ninth
10	ten	10th	tenth
11	eleven	11th	eleventh
12	twelve	12th	twelfth
13	thirteen	13th	thirteenth
14	fourteen	14th	fourteenth
15	fifteen	15th	fifteenth
16	sixteen	16th	sixteenth
17	seventeen	17th	seventeenth
18	eighteen	18th	eighteenth
19	nineteen	19th	nineteenth
20	twenty	20th	twentieth
21	twenty-one	21st	twenty-first
22	twenty-two	22nd	twenty-second
23	twenty-three	23rd	twenty-third
30	thirty	30th	thirtieth
40	forty	40th	fortieth

50	fifty	50th	fiftieth
60	sixty	60th	sixtieth
70	seventy	70th	seventieth
80	eighty	80th	eightieth
90	ninety	90th	ninetieth
100	one hundred	100th	one hundredth
200	two hundred		
1,000	one thousand		
10,000	ten thousand		
100,000	one hundred thousand		
1,000,000	one million		
1,000,000,000	one billion		

Fractions, Decimals and Percentages

	Written	Spoken
Fractions	1/2	one-half
	1/3	one-third
	1/4	one-fourth
	1/5	one-fifth
	1/8	one-eighth
	2/3	two-thirds
	3/4	three-fourths
Decimals	1.0	one point oh
	.75	point seven five
	.6	point six
	2.5	two point five
	0.25	point two five
	.1	point one
Percentages	100%	one hundred percent
	75%	seventy-five percent
	66.6%	sixty-six point six percent
	50%	fifty percent
	33.3%	thirty-three point three percent
	25%	twenty-five percent
	10%	ten percent

Weights and Measures

Length/Distance (English System)

1 foot (ft)	=	12 inches (in)
1 yard (yd)	=	3 feet (or 36 inches)
1 mile (mi)	=	1,760 yards (or 5,280 feet)

Weight

1 pound (lb)	=	16 ounces (oz)
1 ton	=	2,000 pounds

Volume

1 tablespoon (T)	=	3 teaspoons (t)
1 cup (c)	=	16 tablespoons or 8 fluid ounces (fl oz)
1 pint (pt)	=	2 cups
1 quart (qt)	=	2 pints or 4 cups or 32 fluid ounces
1 gallon (gal)	=	4 quarts

Conversion Tables

Length/Distance

From	*To*	*Multiply By*
cm	in	0.3937
in	cm	2.54
m	ft	3.2808
ft	m	0.3048
km	mi	0.6214
mi	km	1.609

Example: 10 cm = 3.94 in (Ten centimeters equals three point nine four inches.)

Weight/Capacity

From	*To*	*Multiply By*
g	oz	0.0353
oz	g	28.35
kg	lb	2.246
lb	kg	0.4536
ml	fl oz	0.0338
fl oz	ml	29.575
l	gal	0.2642
gal	l	3.785

Example: 10 lb = 4.5 kg (Ten pounds equals four point five kilograms.)

Temperature: Celsius (or centigrade) and Fahrenheit

degrees (°) Celsius (C) = 5/9 (degrees Fahrenheit − 32)
degrees (°) Fahrenheit (F) = 9/5 (degrees Celsius + 32)

Examples:

C	100°	30°	25°	20°	15°	10°	5°	0°	−5°
F	212°	86°	77°	68°	59°	50°	41°	32°	23°

Spoken as
84° F   eighty-four degrees Fahrenheit
−8° C   minus eight degrees Celsius

Approximations

nearly   roughly   approximately   about

Examples: There are approximately two and a half centimeters to an inch.
                A kilogram is about 2.2 pounds.

Comparisons

Adjectives: The comparative and superlative forms of adjectives are formed as follows.

(1)   By adding *-er* or *the +-est* to the end of adjectives with one syllable.

	Comparative	**Superlative**
The 486 computer is slow.	The 386 computer is slower.	The 286 is the slowest.
Last year's report was long.	The 2000 report was longer.	This year's report is the longest.

(2)   By adding *more* or *the most* before adjectives with more than one syllable.

	Comparative	**Superlative**
This scanner is reliable.	The XY200 scanner is more reliable.	The XY400 scanner is the most reliable.
Plan A is expensive.	Plan B is more expensive.	Plan C is the most expensive.

(3)   By changing adjectives that end in *-y, -ow,* and *-le* as follows.

funny	funnier	the funniest
easy	easier	the easiest
simple	simpler	the simplest
narrow	narrower	the narrowest

(4)   Note irregular comparatives.

good	better	the best
bad	worse	the worst
far	farther / further	the farthest / the furthest
some	more	the most
little	less	the least

> *Note:*   To add emphasis use *even*.
> Last year's annual report was long, but this year's report is *even* longer.

Adverbs: The comparative and superlative forms of adverbs are formed as follows.

(1)   By adding *-er* and *-est* to the following irregular adverbs.

fast	faster	the fastest
hard	harder	the hardest
late	later	the latest
early	earlier	the earliest

Example: Robert usually works late at the office. Susan works later than Robert, but their boss works the latest of all.

(2)   By adding *more* and *the most* to adverbs that end in *-ly*.

	Comparative	Superlative
Henry works slowly.	Robyn works more slowly than Henry.	Unfortunately, Phillip works the most slowly of all.
Juan speaks English fluently.	Mariko speaks more fluently.	Akira speaks the most fluently of all.

Modifying Comparisons
Use one of the following adverbs before a comparative adjective to indicate the degree of comparison.

Modifying Adverbs

a little	somewhat	significantly
slightly	moderately	much
		remarkably
		considerably
		substantially
		far

Examples: Our profits were better this year than last year.
Our profits were *significantly* better this year.

The Passive Voice

In a passive sentence, the object of an active sentence becomes the subject.

            S   V   O
Active: Robert copied the report.
                S   V   the doer
Passive: The report was copied by Robert.

Forming the Passive

Use a form of the verb *to be* + the Past Participle.

> *Note:* The verb *to be* is in the same tense as the main verb of the active sentence.

	Active Sentence	**Passive Sentence**
Present	Generally speaking, Angela prepares the report.	The report is prepared by Angela.
Present Continuous	The secretary is collating the documents.	The documents are being collated.
Past	The company developed a cure for high blood pressure in 1998.	A cure for high blood pressure was developed in 1998.
Present Perfect	The CEO has assigned a special team to deal with the problem.	A special team has been assigned to deal with the problem.
Past Perfect	The president had commissioned a feasibility study before he implemented the plan.	A feasibility study had been commissioned before the president implemented the plan.
Future	The search committee will appoint a new director next year.	A new director will be appointed next year.

Uses of the Passive

(1) The passive is used when the receiver of the action or the result of the action is emphasized more than the doer.

> *Examples:* A strike was announced.
> Bill was fired.

(2) It is also used to avoid mentioning the doer, either intentionally (a) or because mention of the doer is unnecessary (b).

> *Examples:* A mistake has been made. (a)
> Coffee is grown in Colombia. (b)

(3) It can also be used to emphasize the doer. Often what is mentioned last in a sentence is most memorable.

> *Example:* Microsoft was founded by Bill Gates.

(4) It is used to emphasize a process.

> *Example:* When making steel, iron ore, limestone, and coke are put into a blast furnace. Then the iron is removed from the bottom of the furnace. Next, impurities are removed from the molten iron. After that, the molten steel is made into ingots that are reheated and made into steel slabs.

(5)   It is commonly used in formal communication.

> *Example:*   All carry-on bags must be stored in the compartment above your head.

> *Note:*   Intransitive verbs cannot be made passive:
> *be, seem, appear, sleep, rise, arrive, happen, occur, die*

Review of Verb Tenses

Present Continuous

He is reading a book on management.

  = now

He is reading a lot these days.

  = now in a general sense

He is taking a business trip to the Far East next week.
  = in the future

Simple Present

She usually takes the subway to work.

  = repeated action

Past Continuous

I was talking to him when she called.

  = a long action in the past

  ☐ = was talking
   x = when she called

Simple Past

They talked about investment opportunities.

  = completed past action

Time Expressions

now
past   future   now
right now
today
this evening

now
past   future   these days
lately
currently

now
past   x   future   soon
next week
next month

now
x x x x | x x x x
past   future   usually
every day
all the time

now
x |
past   future   at 3:00
when the phone rang
all morning

now
x |
past   future   yesterday
last week
a week ago

Future

The company <u>will invest</u> in training.
The company <u>is going to invest</u> in training.

    = in the future

now

| x

past   future

soon
next month
in a month

Present Perfect

I <u>have studied</u> finance for several years.

    = from a past time to now

now

past   future

for 6 years
since 1999
all summer

I <u>have visited</u> Sao Paulo twice.

    = repeated past action that can
      be done again in the future

now

x x | [x x]

past   future

several times
once or twice
many times

I <u>have read</u> the newspaper.

    = indefinite past time

now

? |

past   future

already
before now
in the past

Present Perfect Progressive

She has been working in a bank for years.

    = a long past action that will
      probably continue in the future

now

past   future

for years
since 1995
for a long time

Past Perfect

She <u>had left</u> the office before I arrived.

    = the earlier of two past actions
    x = had left
    y = arrived

now

x y |

past   future

earlier
before [that]
before I came

Question Forms with Different Verb Tenses

Present

		She	**goes**	to work at 7:30.
	Does	she	**go**	to work at 7:30?

Yes, she **does.**
[No, she **doesn't.**]

Where	**does**	she	**go**	at 7:30?

To work.

Present Progressive

		She	**is taking** a management course.	
	Is	she	**taking** statistics?	No, she **isn't.** [Yes, she **is.**]
What	**is**	she	**taking?**	Math.

Past

		She	**took** finance last term.	
	Did	she	**take** accounting?	No, she **didn't.** [Yes, she **did.**]
When	**did**	she	**take** finance?	Last semester.

Past Progressive

		He	**was writing** his report when I saw him.	
	Was	he	**writing** his report?	Yes, he **was.** [No, he **wasn't.**]
What	**was**	he	**doing?**	Writing his report.

Future

		She	**will show** our visitors around the plant.	
	Will	she	**show** them around?	Yes, she **will.** [No, she **won't.**]
Who	**will**	she	**show around?**	Our visitors.
		She	**is going to take** a business trip.	
	Is	she	**going to take** a business trip?	Yes, she **is.** [No, she **isn't.**]
What	**is**	she	**going to take?**	A business trip.

Present Perfect

		He	**has gone** to Los Angeles.	
	Has	he	**gone** to Reno?	No, he **hasn't.** [Yes, he **has.**]
Where	**has**	he	**gone?**	To Los Angeles.

Present Perfect Continuous

		He	**has been visiting** our company.	
	Has	he	**been visiting** our company?	Yes, he **has.** [No, he **hasn't.**]
What	has	he	**been visiting?**	Our company.

Past Perfect

		He	**had heard** of me before I met him.	
	Had	he	**heard** of you before you met him?	Yes, he **had.** [No, he **hadn't.**]
When	**had**	he	**heard** of you?	Before I met him.

Past Perfect Continuous

		I	**had been listening** for five minutes when I fell asleep.	
	Had	you	**been listening** carefully?	No, I **hadn't.** [Yes, I **had.**]
How long	**had**	you	**been listening?**	Five minutes.

Future Perfect

		He	**will have finished** by June.	
	Will	he	**have finished** by May?	No, he **won't have.** [Yes, he **will have.**] He **may have.**
When	**will**	he	**have finished?**	By June.

Noncount Nouns

There are two kinds of nouns in English: nouns that we can count (count nouns) and nouns we can't count (noncount nouns). With noncount nouns, *a/an* and plural *-s* are not used.

Count	*Noncount*
a computer	information
computer**s**	

Most nouns are countable and can be used with countable expressions of quantity; noncount nouns have their own expressions of quantity.

Count

large quantity

↑ a great many computers
| a large number of computers
| many computers / a lot of computers
| some / five / several computers
| a few computers
| not many computers
↓ few computers

small quantity

Noncount

a great deal of information
a large amount of information
a lot of information
some information
a little information
not much information
little information

Categories of Noncount Nouns

Abstract Nouns

advice	experience	inflation	nonsense	research
anger	fun	information	patience	tolerance
competition	happiness	intelligence	progress	trouble
confusion	harm	knowledge	quality	unemployment
courage	help	leisure	recreation	violence
enjoyment	independence	luck	relaxation	work

Materials

bread	dirt	gold	meat
bronze	earth	graphite	sand
coal	fish	iron	steel
cement	glass	leather	wood

Things with Many Pieces		**Things That Need a Container**		
cereal	hair	butter	ice cream	oil
corn	hay	coffee	juice	water
dust	pasta	gas	milk	wine
grass	rice			

Generic

architecture	clothing	jewelry	merchandise
beef	education	junk	money
behavior	equipment	luggage	seafood
cheese	fruit	machinery	trade
commerce	furniture	mail	wildlife

Business Etiquette Quiz

Decide whether these statements about behaviors in the United States are true or false.

	TRUE	FALSE
1. In the United States it is best to shake a person's hand with a light touch.	❑	❑
2. When you are introduced, it's best to look the other person directly in the eyes.	❑	❑
3. In business situations, people always use first names right away.	❑	❑
4. Business women generally use the title *Ms.*	❑	❑
5. If you are the senior person, you are the one who invites the use of first names.	❑	❑
6. The usual custom is to use titles (*Mr., Ms.*) with first names.	❑	❑
7. When listening to presentations, North American audiences prefer long, well-developed introductions that provide a lot of background before getting to the point.	❑	❑
8. It is helpful to write out your presentation word for word so that you can memorize it easily.	❑	❑
9. When presenting your points visually, it is important to use large type and put only two or three points on each slide or transparency.	❑	❑
10. When presenting quantitative information, include as many facts and figures as possible.	❑	❑
11. When telephoning a business contact, it is important to begin by clearly stating the purpose of your call.	❑	❑
12. It is common to call people at home about business matters in North America.	❑	❑
13. When making an appointment on the telephone, it is advisable to restate the date, time, and place of the appointment at the end of the call.	❑	❑
14. If you are giving a presentation at a company, feel free to pass out business cards in the beginning to those in attendance so they will know who you are.	❑	❑
15. Pass out your business cards freely to everyone you meet and invite people to pass your card on to others.	❑	❑
16. A junior executive should wait until a more senior executive asks for his or her business card.	❑	❑
17. In the United States it is best to take plenty of time to explain yourself fully during a discussion. There's no point in leaving something out.	❑	❑

18. Because people in the United States are very informal, it's best to approach an important discussion with informality. It's not a good idea to develop your arguments and ideas in advance because you may sound artificial. ❏ ❏

19. As in many places in the world, in the United States people enjoy friendly business relationships. For this reason, together with the informality, it is less important to have facts to support your point of view. ❏ ❏

20. People in the United States typically like to have all the background information to consider first before making a decision. ❏ ❏

Multiple Choice

Answer by circling the letter of your choice. Sometimes there will be more than one answer.

1. Circle any of the following points that are typical of business presentations in North America.

   a. The speaker usually reads from a printed text.
   b. Eye contact with the audience is important.
   c. The audience often interacts with the speaker and asks questions.
   d. The speaker typically works from an outline to follow a logical progression.
   e. Personal interest stories and humor are common.
   f. The speaker stands in one place while giving the presentation.

2. If you don't understand what someone said on the phone, you could say any of the following.

   a. What did you say?
   b. Huh?
   c. Excuse me, would you mind repeating that?
   d. I'm sorry, I didn't understand what you said.

3. It is advisable to return calls

   a. within one week.
   b. within a month.
   c. within 24 hours.
   d. whenever you have time.

4. If you are at a business reception, cards are usually exchanged

   a. when you are first introduced to someone.
   b. in the middle of the conversation.
   c. at the end of a conversation when some business is discussed.

5. At a social dinner

   a. business is discussed at the beginning of the meal.
   b. business is discussed at the end of the meal.
   c. business is discussed throughout the meal.
   d. business-related discussions are generally avoided during the meal.

6. When you arrive at the restaurant, you should tell the receptionist

   a. I sure am hungry. I wish I had a reservation.
   b. We've got a reservation.
   c. I would like to make a reservation, please.

7. What is a "special"?

   a. Especially good service at a restaurant
   b. A dish prepared for the day
   c. Valet parking where someone parks your car for you

8. How often do people in the United States drink wine with a nice dinner out?

   a. Not that often
   b. Usually just with seafood
   c. Frequently

9. If you order the wine, who will taste it to make sure it's good?

   a. The person who orders it
   b. It's polite to let your dinner companion taste it first.
   c. The waitperson will taste it for you.

10. What should you do if you don't know much about wine?

    a. Ask the waitperson for a recommendation.
    b. Just order anything. It will be fine.
    c. Don't ask your guests if they want wine so that you don't have to order it

11. If the service is good, how much should the tip be?

    a. 15–20%
    b. 10%
    c. 10–15%

12. What is a gratuity?

    a. A kind of shellfish
    b. An extra service in a restaurant
    c. A tip